Anonymous

School Lyrics

Sacred hymns

Anonymous

School Lyrics
Sacred hymns

ISBN/EAN: 9783744794121

Printed in Europe, USA, Canada, Australia, Japan

Cover: Foto ©Paul-Georg Meister /pixelio.de

More available books at **www.hansebooks.com**

PREFACE.

THE simple object of the compiler of this little book has been to prepare a convenient, compact, and select manual of hymns for use in the school-room and the family circle. The evident want of such a book, and repeated and unavailing search for one, first suggested the idea of preparing it. Great labor and care have been bestowed upon it, particularly in the choice and arrangement of the hymns. Out of several thousand examined carefully, about two hundred and sixty have been selected on account of their special fitness for devotional exercises in schools.

Among the points of excellence which the compiler has aimed to secure are the following:

1. To have *nothing superfluous* in the book. It is believed that all the hymns in this collection can be used in the school-room, either on ordinary or special occasions. As it is rare that more than three or four stanzas are sung at once, an effort has been made to strike out the more unimportant ones, except where the continuity of thought would be thereby interrupted.

2. To select only the *choicest standard* hymns, including many of the old and established favorites. The book has been particularly designed for schools of a higher grade, and yet the compiler's experience has led him to believe that the best lyric hymns of the language can be appre-

ciated even by children; and when these are lodged in the memory by frequent repetition, they become a valuable possession for a lifetime.

3. To include only hymns which are *unsectarian* in their character, such as can be used by religious persons of any Christian denomination.

4. To have, for the most part, only *hymns of true devotion*, tributes of gratitude and praise, petitions for divine favor, etc. Didactic and hortatory hymns, however, have not been entirely excluded.

5. To introduce a *variety of metres*, so as to afford full scope for a school choir, or for schools where instruction in music is given. A book on a more extensive plan, embracing both hymns and tunes, was meditated at first; but as sacred tunes are so easily caught up and retained by the young, and as they so soon weary of any thing stereotyped and fixed in the combination of hymns and tunes, it was felt that such a book would not meet the present wide-spread and pressing want so much as a cheap, condensed, and handy little manual—a sort of pocket hymn-book.

Respecting the importance of this part of school exercises and their happy effect, not only upon the character of the pupils, but upon the general discipline of a school, there can be no question, probably, among teachers of experience. The compiler hopes that he may have contributed somewhat to the greater usefulness and the better enjoyment of the hour of school devotions. S. M. CAPRON.

HARTFORD, *July* 1, 1868.

TABLE OF CONTENTS.

		HYMN
1.	Morning and Evening Devotions: Opening and Close of School...............	1–29
2.	Praise and Thanksgiving...............	30–54
3.	Works and Attributes of God..........	55–101
4.	Holy Scriptures.......................	102–106
5.	Jesus Christ, Birth, Life, etc...........	107–144
6.	Various Petitions, Prayer..............	145–200
7.	Religious Duties and Privileges........	201–220
8.	Special Occasions.....................	221–231
9.	Mortality and Immortality.............	232–266

		PAGE
10.	Chants................................	153
11.	Index of First Lines...................	157

SCHOOL LYRICS.

MORNING AND EVENING DEVOTIONS.

1. *Morning Hymn.* 6s. & 4s.

GOD of the morning ray,
God of the rising day,
  Glorious in power!
In thee we live and move,
And thus we daily prove
Thy condescending love
  Each passing hour.

2 God of our feeble race,
God of redeeming grace,
  Spirit all-blest!
Our own eternal Friend,
Thy guardian influence lend,
From every snare defend—
  In thee we rest.   HASTINGS.

2. *Morning.* C. M.

ONCE more, my soul, the rising day
  Salutes thy waking eyes;
Once more, my voice, thy tribute pay
  To Him that rules the skies.

2 'Tis he supports my mortal frame;
  My tongue shall speak his praise;

My sins would rouse his wrath to flame,
  And yet his wrath delays.

3 Great God, let all my hours be thine,
  While I enjoy the light;
Then shall my sun in smiles decline,
  And bring a pleasant night.   WATTS.

3.   Psalm xix. 5, 8.   L. M.

GOD of the morning, at thy voice
  The cheerful sun makes haste to rise,
And like a giant doth rejoice
  To run his journey through the skies.

2 Oh, like the sun, may I fulfill
  Th' appointed duties of the day;
With ready mind and active will
  March on, and keep my heavenly way.

3 Give me thy counsel for my guide,
  And then receive me to thy bliss;
All my desires and hopes beside
  Are faint and cold, compared with this.
                                WATTS.

4.   *The Morning Sacrifice.*   L. M.

AWAKE, my soul, and with the sun
  Thy daily stage of duty run;
Shake off dull sloth, and joyful rise
To pay thy morning sacrifice.

2 Lord, I my vows to thee renew:
Scatter my sins as morning dew;
Guard my first springs of thought and will.
And with thyself my spirit fill.

3 Direct, control, suggest, this day,
All I design, or do, or say;
That all my powers, with all their might,
In thy sole glory may unite. KENN.

5. *Isaiah xxxiii. 2.* 7s.

NOW the shades of night are gone;
Now the morning light is come;
Lord, may we be thine to-day!
Drive the shades of sin away.

2 Fill our souls with heavenly light,
Banish doubt, and clear our sight;
In thy service, Lord, to-day,
May we stand, and watch and pray.

3 When our work of life is past,
Oh, receive us then at last;
Night and sin will be no more,
When we reach the heavenly shore.

6. *Morning Prayer.* C. M.

LORD! in the morning thou shalt hear
  My voice ascending high;
To thee will I direct my prayer,
  To thee lift up mine eye.

2 Thou art a God before whose sight
  The wicked shall not stand;
Sinners shall ne'er be thy delight,
  Nor dwell at thy right hand.

3 Oh, may thy Spirit guide my feet
  In ways of righteousness!
Make every path of duty straight,
  And plain before my face. WATTS.

7.   Lam. iii. 22, 23.   7s.

IN the morning I will pray
  For God's blessing on the day;
What this day shall be my lot,
Light or darkness, know I not.

2 Should it be with clouds o'ercast,
Clouds of sorrow, gathering fast,
Thou, who givest light divine,
Shine within me, Lord, oh shine!

3 Show me, if I tempted be,
How to find all strength in thee,
And a perfect triumph win
Over every bosom sin.

4 Keep my feet from secret snares,
Keep mine eyes, O God, from tears!
Every step thy love attend,
And my soul from death defend!
                               FURNESS.

8.   *Consecration.*   8s. 7s. & 4s.

WHILE our days on earth are lengthened,
    May we give them, Lord, to thee;
Cheered by hope, and daily strengthened,
  May we run, nor weary be,
      Till thy glory,
  Without cloud, in heaven we see.

2 There, in worship purer, sweeter,
  All thy children shall adore;
Tasting of enjoyment greater
  Than they could conceive before;
      Full enjoyment—
  Full and pure for evermore.   KELLY.

MORNING.

9.   *Daily Obedience.*   L. M.

FORTH in thy name, O Lord, we go,
  Our daily labor to pursue;
Thee, only thee, resolved to know,
  In all we think, or speak, or do.

2 Still would we bear thy easy yoke,
  And every moment watch and pray;
Would still to things eternal look,
  And hasten to thy glorious day.

3 For thee alone we would employ
  Whate'er thy bounteous grace has given;
Would run our course with even joy,
  And closely walk with thee to heaven.
                            C. WESLEY.

10.   *Opening of School.*   7s.

SUPPLIANT, lo, thy children bend,
  Father, for thy blessing now;
Thou canst teach us, guide, defend;
  We are weak, almighty thou.

2 With the peace thy word imparts,
  Be the taught and teachers blessed;
In our lives, and in our hearts,
  Father, be thy laws impressed.

3 Pour into each longing mind
  Light and pardon from above,
Charity for all our kind,
  Trusting faith, and holy love.

11.   *Morning Prayer.*   C. M.

NOW that the sun is gleaming bright,
  Implore we, bending low,

That He, the uncreated light,
　May guide us as we go.

2 No sinful word, nor deed of wrong,
　Nor thoughts that idly rove;
But simple truth be on our tongue,
　And in our hearts be love.

3 And grant that to thine honor, Lord,
　Our daily toil may tend;
That we begin it at thy word,
　And in thy favor end.

12.　　　　*Daily Mercies.*　　　　L. M.

MY God, how endless is thy love!
　Thy gifts are every evening new;
And morning mercies, from above,
　Gently distill, like early dew.

2 Thou spread'st the curtains of the night,
　Great Guardian of my sleeping hours!
Thy sovereign word restores the light,
　And quickens all my drowsy powers.

3 I yield my powers to thy command;
　To thee I consecrate my days:
Perpetual blessings from thy hand
　Demand perpetual songs of praise.

　　　　　　　　　　　　WATTS.

13.　　　*God's Blessing sought.*　　8s. & 7s.

GRACIOUS God, our Heavenly Father!
　Meet and bless our school, we pray;
As in humble trust we gather,
　Teachers, scholars, here to-day.
Every joy and every blessing
　From thy bounteous hand we own;

May thy love, our souls possessing,
  Draw us nearer to thy throne.

2 Weak, imperfect, tempted, erring,
  From thy precepts, Lord, we stray;
Let thy spirit, from our wandering,
  Bring us back to virtue's way.
Humble, penitent, confiding,
  May we rest our hope in thee;
In thy favor, Lord, abiding,
  In thy peace and purity.

14. Lam. iii. 23. L. M.

NEW every morning is the love
  Our wakening and uprising prove;
Through sleep and darkness safely brought,
Restored to life, and power, and thought.

2 New mercies, each returning day,
Hover around us while we pray;
New perils past, new sins forgiven,
New thoughts of God, new hopes of heaven.

3 If on our daily course our mind
Be set to hallow all we find,
New treasures still, of countless price,
God will provide for sacrifice.

4 The trivial round, the common task
Will furnish all we need to ask,
Room to deny ourselves, a road
To bring us daily nearer God.

5 Only, O Lord, in thy dear love,
Fit us for perfect rest above;
And help us, this and every day,
To live more nearly as we pray. KEBLE.

15. *Evening.* C. M.

HAIL, tranquil hour of closing day!
  Begone, disturbing care!
And look, my soul, from earth away,
  To Him who heareth prayer.

2 How sweet to look, in thoughtful hope,
  Beyond this fading sky,
And hear him call his children up
  To his fair home on high.

3 Calmly the day forsakes our heaven
  To dawn beyond the west;
So let my soul, in life's last even,
  Retire to glorious rest.   L. BACON.

16. *Evening Prayer.* 6s. & 4s.

FATHER of love and power,
  Guard thou our evening hour,
    Shield with thy might:
For all thy care this day
Our grateful thanks we pay,
And to our Father pray,
    Bless us to-night.

2 Jesus, Immanuel,
Come in thy love to dwell
    In hearts contrite:
For many sins we grieve,
But we thy grace receive,
And in thy word believe;
    Bless us to-night.

17. *Prayer for Protection.* 8s. 7s. & 7s.

THRO' the day thy love has spared us,
  Soon are we to seek our rest;

Through the silent watches guard us,
  Let no foe our peace molest.
Jesus, thou our guardian be,
Sweet it is to trust in thee.

2 Pilgrims here on earth, and strangers,
  Dwelling in the midst of foes;
Us and ours preserve from dangers,
  In thine arms may we repose.
And, when life's sad day is past,
Rest with thee in heaven at last. KELLY.

18. *Prayer for Forgiveness.* 7s.

SOFTLY now the light of day
  Fades upon my sight away;
Free from care, from labor free,
Lord, I would commune with thee.

2 Thou, whose all-pervading eye
Naught escapes without, within,
Pardon each infirmity,
Open fault, and secret sin.

3 Soon, for me, the light of day
Shall forever pass away:
Then, from sin and sorrow free,
Take me, Lord, to dwell with thee.
           DOANE.

19. *Evening Prayer.* 7s.

THOU, from whom we never part,
  Thou, whose love is every where,
Thou, who seest every heart,
  Listen to our evening prayer.

2 Father, fill our hearts with love,
  Love unfailing, full and free;

Love that no alarm can move,
　　　　Love that ever rests on thee.

　　3 Heavenly Father! through the night
　　　　Keep us safe from every ill;
　　　Cheerful as the morning light,
　　　　May we wake to do thy will.

20. *Protecting Care.* P. M.

GOD, that madest earth and heaven,
　　Darkness and light!
Who the day for toil hast given,
　　For rest the night!
May thine angel guards defend us,
Slumbers sweet thy mercy send us,
Holy dreams and hopes attend us,
　　This livelong night!

2 Guard us waking, guard us sleeping;
　　And, when we die,
May we in thy mighty keeping
　　All peaceful lie;
When the last dread call shall wake us,
Do not thou our God forsake us,
But to reign in glory take us,
　　With thee on high.　　　HEBER.

21. *Evening Song.* 7s.

O my Saviour, guardian true,
　　All my life is thine to keep;
At thy feet my work I do,
　　In thine arms I fall asleep.

2 Leaning on thy tender care,
　　Thou hast led my soul aright;
Fervent was my morning prayer;
　　Joyful is my song to-night.

3 Tender mercies on my way
  Falling softly like the dew,
Sent me freshly every day—
  I will bless the Lord for you.

4 Source of all that comforts me,
  Well of joy for which I long;
Let the song I sing to thee,
  Be an everlasting song!

22. *The Evening Blessing.* 8s. & 7s.

SAVIOUR, breathe an evening blessing,
  Ere repose our spirits seal:
Sin and want we come confessing;
  Thou canst save, and thou canst heal.

2 Though destruction walk around us,
  Though the arrow near us fly,
Angel-guards from thee surround us;
  We are safe, if thou art nigh.

3 Though the night be dark and dreary,
  Darkness can not hide from thee:
Thou art he who, never weary,
  Watcheth where thy people be.

4 Should swift death this night o'ertake us,
  And our couch become our tomb,
May the morn in heaven awake us,
  Clad in light and deathless bloom.
                             EDMESTON.

23. Luke xxiv. 29. L. M.

SUN of my soul! thou Saviour dear,
  It is not night if thou be near;
Oh, may no earth-born cloud arise,
  To hide thee from thy servant's eyes.

B

2 When the soft dews of kindly sleep
  My wearied eyelids gently keep,
Be my last thought—how sweet to rest
  Forever on my Saviour's breast.

3 Abide with me from morn till eve,
  For without thee I can not live;
Abide with me when night is nigh,
  For without thee I dare not die.

4 Come near and bless us when we wake,
  Ere thro' the world our way we take;
Till in the ocean of thy love
  We lose ourselves in heaven above.
KEBLE.

24.   Luke xxiv. 29.   10s.

ABIDE with me! fast falls the eventide,
  The darkness deepens; Lord, with me abide!
When other helpers fail, and comforts flee,
Help of the helpless, oh, abide with me!

2 Swift to its close ebbs out life's little day;
Earth's joys grow dim, its glories pass away;
Change and decay in all around I see;
O thou, who changest not, abide with me!

3 I need thy presence every passing hour;
What but thy grace can foil the tempter's power?
Who like thyself my guide and stay can be?
Through cloud and sunshine, oh, abide with me!
LYTE.

25.   *Abiding in God.*   S. M.

STILL with thee, O my God,
  I would desire to be;
By day, by night, at home, abroad,
  I would be still with thee.

OPENING AND CLOSE OF SCHOOL.

2 With thee, when dawn comes in,
   And calls me back to care;
Each day returning to begin
   With thee, my God, in prayer.

3 With thee, when day is done,
   And evening calms the mind:
The setting as the rising sun
   With thee my heart would find:

4 With thee, in thee, by faith
   Abiding I would be;
By day, by night, in life, in death,
   I would be still with thee.

26.   *Opening of a Term.*   C. M.

SHINE on our souls, eternal God,
   With rays of beauty shine;
Oh let thy favor crown our days,
   And all their round be thine.

2 With thee let every week begin,
   With thee each day be spent,
For thee each fleeting hour employed,
   Since each by thee is lent.

3 Thus cheer us through this desert road,
   Till all our labors cease;
And heaven refresh our weary souls
   With everlasting peace.   DODDRIDGE.

27.   *Close of School.*   7s.

FOR a season called to part,
   Let us now ourselves commend
To the gracious eye and heart
   Of our ever present Friend.

2 Jesus! hear our humble prayer;
   Tender Shepherd of thy sheep!
Let thy mercy and thy care
   All our souls in safety keep.

3 Then if thou thy help afford,
   Joyful songs to thee shall rise,
And our souls shall praise the Lord,
   Who regards our humble cries.
                              NEWTON.

28.   *Close of a Term.*   L. M.

THY presence, everlasting God,
   Wide o'er all nature spreads abroad;
Thy watchful eyes, which can not sleep,
In every place thy children keep.

2 While near each other we remain,
Thou dost our lives and souls sustain;
When absent, Father, let us share
Thy smiles, thy counsels, and thy care.

3 To thee we all our ways commit,
And seek our comforts near thy feet;
Still on our souls vouchsafe to shine,
And guard and guide us still as thine.

4 Permit us, Lord, within this house,
Again to pay our grateful vows;
Or if that joy no more be known,
Then may we meet around thy throne.
                              DODDRIDGE.

29.   *Closing Hymn.*   L. M.

FATHER, once more let grateful praise
   And humble prayer to thee ascend;
Thou Guide and Guardian of our ways,
   Our early and our only Friend.

2 Since every day and hour that's gone
  Has been with mercy richly crowned,
Mercy, we know, shall still flow on,
  Forever sure, as time rolls round.

3 Hear, then, the parting prayers we pour,
  And bind our hearts in love alone;
And if we meet on earth no more,
  May we at last surround thy throne.

PRAISE AND THANKSGIVING.

30. *The Voice of Praise.* C. M.

LIFT up to God the voice of praise,
  Whose breath our souls inspired;
Loud and more loud the anthems raise,
  With grateful ardor fired.

2 Lift up to God the voice of praise,
  Whose goodness, passing thought,
Loads every moment, as it flies,
  With benefits unsought.

3 Lift up to God the voice of praise,
  For hope's transporting ray,
Which lights through darkest shades of death
  To realms of endless day. WARDLAW.

31. *Praise the Lord.* 8s. & 7s.

PRAISE the Lord; ye heavens, adore him;
  Praise him, angels in the height;
Sun and moon, rejoice before him;
  Praise him, all ye stars of light.

2 Praise the Lord, for he hath spoken;
　　Worlds his mighty voice obeyed;
Laws, which never can be broken,
　　For their guidance he hath made.

3 Praise the Lord, for he is glorious;
　　Never shall his promise fail;
God hath made his saints victorious;
　　Sin and death shall not prevail.

32. *Praise to Jehovah.* 8s. & 7s.

PRAISE to thee, thou great Creator!
　　Praise to thee from every tongue:
Join, my soul, with every creature,
　　Join the universal song.

2 Father, Source of all compassion,
　　Pure, unbounded grace is thine:
Hail the God of our salvation!
　　Praise him for his love divine.

3 For ten thousand blessings given,
　　For the hope of future joy,
Sound his praise thro' earth and heaven,
　　Sound Jehovah's praise on high.

4 Joyfully on earth adore him,
　　Till in heaven our song we raise;
There, enraptured, fall before him,
　　Lost in wonder, love, and praise.
　　　　　　　　　　　FAWCETT.

33. Psalm cxxxvi. L. M.

GIVE to our God immortal praise;
　Mercy and truth are all his ways:
Wonders of grace to God belong;
Repeat his mercies in your song.

2 Give to the Lord of lords renown,
The King of kings with glory crown:
His mercies ever shall endure,
When lords and kings are known no more.

3 He built the earth, he spread the sky,
And fixed the starry lights on high:
Wonders of grace to God belong;
Repeat his mercies in your song.

4 Through this vain world he guides our feet,
And leads us to his heavenly seat:
His mercies ever shall endure,
When this vain world shall be no more.
WATTS.

34. *Gratitude.* 7s.

PRAISE to God, immortal praise,
  For the love that crowns our days;
Bounteous Source of every joy!
Let thy praise our tongues employ.

2 All that spring with bounteous hand
Scatters o'er the smiling land;
All that liberal autumn pours
From her rich o'erflowing stores;

3 Lord, for these our souls shall raise
Grateful vows, and solemn praise:
And when every blessing's flown,
Love thee for thyself alone.   BARBAULD.

35. Psalm cl. 7s. & 6s.

PRAISE the Lord, who reigns above,
  And keeps his courts below;
Praise him for his boundless love,
  And all his greatness show!

Praise him for his noble deeds;
  Praise him for his matchless power;
Him, from whom all good proceeds,
  Let earth and heaven adore.

2 Him, in whom they move and live,
  Let every creature sing;
Glory to our Saviour give,
  And homage to our King:
Hallowed be his name beneath,
  As in heaven, on earth adored;
Praise the Lord in every breath,
  Let all things praise the Lord.

36. *Glory of God.* 8s. & 7s.

BLEST be thou, O God of Israel!
  Thou, our Father and our Lord!
Majesty is thine forever;
  Ever be thy name adored.

2 Thine, O Lord, are power and greatness;
  Glory, victory, are thine own;
All is thine in earth or heaven,
  Over all thy boundless throne.

3 Riches come of thee, and honor;
  Power and might to thee belong;
Thine it is to make us prosper,
  Only thine to make us strong.

4 Lord, our God, for these, thy bounties,
  Hymns of gratitude we raise;
To thy name, forever glorious,
  Ever we address our praise.

37. *Thanksgiving.* 8s. & 7s.

PRAISE the Lord, when blushing morning
  Wakes the blossoms fresh with dew,

Praise him when revived creation
  Beams with beauties fair and new.

2 Praise the Lord, when early breezes
  Come so fragrant from the flowers,
Praise, thou willow, by the brook-side,
  Praise, ye birds, among the bowers.

3 Praise the Lord, and may his blessing
  Guide us in the way of truth,
Keep our feet from paths of error,
  Make us holy in our youth.

38.   *Praise from all Lands.*   7s.

ALL ye nations, praise the Lord;
  All ye lands, your voices raise;
Heaven and earth, with loud accord,
  Praise the Lord, forever praise.

2 For his truth and mercy stand,
  Past, and present, and to be,
Like the years of his right hand,
  Like his own eternity.

3 Praise him, ye who know his love;
  Praise him from the depths beneath;
Praise him in the heights above;
  Praise your Maker, all that breathe.
                    MONTGOMERY.

39.   *Adoration.*   7s.

HEAVENLY Father, sovereign Lord,
  Be thy glorious name adored!
Lord, thy mercies never fail;
Hail, celestial Goodness, hail!

2 Though unworthy, Lord, thine ear
Deign our humble songs to hear;

Purer praise we hope to bring,
When around thy throne we sing.

3 While on earth ordained to stay,
Guide our footsteps in thy way,
Till we come to dwell with thee,
Till we all thy glory see.

40. *Praise.* 6s. & 4s.

COME, thou almighty King,
Help us thy name to sing,
 Help us to praise!
Father all glorious,
O'er all victorious,
Come, and reign over us,
 Ancient of Days!

2 Jesus, our Lord, descend;
From all our foes defend,
 Nor let us fall;
Let thine almighty aid
Our sure defense be made,
Our souls on thee be stayed:
 Lord, hear our call! MADAN.

41. Psalm cxlviii. C. P. M.

BEGIN, my soul, th' exalted lay;
Let each enraptured thought obey,
 And praise th' Almighty's name:
Lo! heaven and earth, and seas and skies,
In one melodious concert rise,
 To swell th' inspiring theme.

2 Ye angels, catch the thrilling sound,
While all th' adoring throngs around
 His boundless mercy sing:
Let every listening saint above

Wake all the tuneful soul of love,
  And touch the sweetest string.

3 Let every element rejoice;
Ye thunders, burst with awful voice
  To him who bids you roll:
His praise in softer notes declare,
Each whispering breeze of yielding air,
  And breathe it to the soul.

4 Let man, by nobler passions swayed,
Let man, in God's own image made,
  His breath in praise employ:
Spread wide his Maker's name around,
While heaven's broad arch rings back the sound,
  The song of holy joy!   OGILVIE.

42.   Psalm cxlv.   L. M.

MY God, my King, thy various praise
  Shall fill the remnant of my days;
Thy grace employ my humble tongue,
Till death and glory raise the song.

2 The wings of every hour shall bear
Some thankful tribute to thine ear;
And every setting sun shall see
New works of duty done for thee.

3 But who can speak thy wondrous deeds?
Thy greatness all our thoughts exceeds;
Vast and unsearchable thy ways!
Vast and immortal be thy praise! WATTS.

43.   *Delight in Praise.*   C. M.

YES, I will bless thee, O my God!
  Through all my earthly days;

And to eternity prolong
  Thy vast, thy boundless praise.

2 In every smiling, happy hour,
  Be this my sweet employ:
Thy praise refines my earthly bliss,
  And doubles all my joy.

3 When gloomy care and keen distress
  Afflict my throbbing breast,
Thy praise shall mingle with my tears,
  And lull each pain to rest.

4 Nor shall my tongue alone proclaim
  The honors of my God;
My life, with all its active powers,
  Shall spread thy praise abroad.

HEGINBOTHAM.

44. *The God of Spring.* 7s. 6l.

PRAISE and thanks and cheerful love
  Rise from every thing below,
To the mighty One above,
  Who his wondrous love doth show:
Praise him, each created thing!—
God, your Father! God of spring!

2 Praise him, trees so lately bare!
  Praise him, fresh and new-born flowers!
All ye creatures of the air,
  All ye soft-descending showers,
Praise, with each awakening thing,
Praise your Maker—God of spring!

3 Praise him, man!—thy fitful heart
  Let this balmy season move
To employ its noblest part,
  Softest mercy, sweetest love—

Blessing, with each living thing,
God the bounteous—God of spring!

45. *Song of Praise.* 6s. & 4s.

GLAD hearts to thee we bring,
　With joy thy name we sing,
　　Father above!
Creation praises thee,
On all around we see
　　Tokens of love.

2 Giver of all our powers!
Now, in life's morning hours,
　　May they be thine!
Pure and from error free,
An offering worthy thee,
　　Father Divine!

46. *The Throne of Love.* C. M.

COME, let us lift our joyful eyes
　Up to the courts above,
And smile to see our Father there,
　Upon a throne of love.

2 The peaceful gates of heavenly bliss
　Are opened by the Son;
High let us raise our notes of praise,
　And reach th' almighty throne.

3 To thee ten thousand thanks we bring,
　Great Advocate on high;
And glory to th' eternal King,
　Who lays his anger by. WATTS.

47. *Thanksgiving.* H. M.

GIVE thanks to God most high,
　The universal Lord,

The sovereign King of kings;
    And be his name adored:
  Thy mercy, Lord, | And ever sure
  Shall still endure; | Abides thy word.

  2 How mighty is his hand!
    What wonders hath he done!
  He formed the earth and seas,
    And spread the heavens alone:
  His power and grace | And let his name
  Are still the same; | Have endless praise.

  3 Give thanks aloud to God,
    To God, the heavenly King;
  And let the spacious earth
    His works and glories sing:
  Thy mercy, Lord, | And ever sure
  Shall still endure; | Abides thy word.
                                    WATTS.

48.   *Praise a Pleasure.*   L. M.

SWEET is the work, my God, my King,
  To praise thy name, give thanks, and sing;
To show thy love by morning light,
And talk of all thy truth at night.

2 My heart shall triumph in my Lord,
And bless his works, and bless his word;
Thy works of grace, how bright they shine!
How deep thy counsels! how divine!

3 When shall I see, and hear, and know
All I desired or wished below,
And every power find sweet employ
In an eternal world of joy?   WATTS.

49.   Psalm xcv.   S. M.

COME, sound his praise abroad,
  And hymns of glory sing;
Jehovah is the sovereign God,
  The universal King.

2 He formed the deeps unknown;
  He gave the seas their bound;
The watery worlds are all his own,
  And all the solid ground.

3 Come, worship at his throne,
  Come, bow before the Lord:
We are his work and not our own;
  He formed us by his word.   WATTS.

50.   *Bless the Lord.*   S. M.

OH, bless the Lord, my soul!
  His grace to thee proclaim;
And all that is within me join
  To bless his holy name.

2 Oh, bless the Lord, my soul!
  His mercies bear in mind;
Forget not all his benefits:
  The Lord to thee is kind.

3 He pardons all thy sins,
  Prolongs thy feeble breath;
He healeth thy infirmities,
  And ransoms thee from death.

4 Then bless his holy name,
  Whose grace hath made thee whole;
Whose loving kindness crowns thy days:
  Oh, bless the Lord, my soul!
                MONTGOMERY.

51. *Joy in God's Providence.* 7s.

THOU, who dwell'st enthroned above;
Thou, in whom we live and move;
Thou, who art most great, most high—
God from all eternity!

2 Oh, how sweet, how excellent
When all tongues and hearts consent,
Grateful hearts, and joyful tongues,
Hymning thee in tuneful songs!

3 When the morning paints the skies,
When the stars of evening rise,
We thy praises will record,
Sovereign Ruler, mighty Lord! SANDYS.

52. *God only Wise.* L. M.

AWAKE, my tongue, thy tribute bring
To Him who gave thee power to sing:
Praise Him, who has all praise above,
The Source of wisdom and of love.

2 Through each bright world above, behold
Ten thousand thousand charms unfold;
Earth, air, and mighty seas combine,
To speak his wisdom, all divine.

3 But in redemption, oh, what grace!
Its wonders, oh, what thought can trace!
Here wisdom shines forever bright:
Praise Him, my soul, with sweet delight.
NEEDHAM.

53. *The Glory of God.* L. M.

COME, O my soul! in sacred lays
Attempt thy great Creator's praise:

But, oh, what tongue can speak his fame!
What mortal verse can reach the theme!

2 Enthroned amid the radiant spheres,
He glory like a garment wears;
To form a robe of light divine,
Ten thousand suns around him shine.

3 In all our Maker's grand designs,
Almighty power, with wisdom, shines;
His works, thro' all this wondrous frame,
Declare the glory of his name.

4 Raised on devotion's lofty wing,
Do thou, my soul, his glories sing;
And let his praise employ thy tongue,
Till listening worlds shall join the song.
BLACKLOCK.

54. *The Lord is King.* L. M.

THE Lord is King! lift up thy voice,
O earth, and all ye heavens, rejoice!
From world to world the joy shall ring:
"The Lord omnipotent is King!"

2 The Lord is King! who then shall dare
Resist his will, distrust his care?
Holy and true are all his ways:
Let every creature speak his praise.

3 Oh, when his wisdom can mistake,
His might decay, his love forsake,
Then may his children cease to sing
"The Lord omnipotent is King."
CONDER.

WORKS AND ATTRIBUTES OF GOD.

55. *Omnipotence.* C. M.

JEHOVAH, God! thy gracious power
  On every hand we see;
Oh, may the blessings of each hour
  Lead all our thoughts to thee!

2 If, on the wings of morn, we speed
  To earth's remotest bound,
Thy hand will there our footsteps lead,
  Thy love our path surround.

3 Thy power is in the ocean deeps,
  And reaches to the skies;
Thine eye of mercy never sleeps,
  Thy goodness never dies.

4 In all the varying scenes of time,
  On thee our hopes depend;
Through every age, in every clime,
  Our Father, and our Friend.
                          THOMSON.

56. *Works of God.* C. P. M.

THY mighty working, mighty God!
  Wakes all my powers; I look abroad,
    And can no longer rest;
I, too, must sing when all things sing,
And from my heart the praises ring
    The Highest loveth best.

2 If thou, in thy great love to us,
Wilt scatter joy and beauty thus
    O'er this poor earth of ours;

What nobler glories shall be given
Hereafter in thy shining heaven,
  Set round with golden towers!

3 What thrilling joy, when on our sight
Christ's garden beams in cloudless light
  Where all the air is sweet;
Still laden with th' unwearied hymn
From all the thousand seraphim
  Who God's high praise repeat!

4 Oh, were I there! oh, that I now
Before thy throne, my God, could bow,
  And bear my heavenly palm!
Then, like the angels, would I raise
My voice, and sing thine endless praise
  In many a sweet-toned psalm.

57. Psalm xviii. 11. 10s. & 11s.

OH, worship the King all-glorious above,
  And gratefully sing his wonderful love;
Our Shield and Defender, the Ancient of Days,
Pavilioned in splendor, and girded with praise.

2 Oh, tell of his might, and sing of his grace,
Whose robe is the light, whose canopy space;
His chariots of wrath the deep thunder-clouds form,
And dark is his path on the wings of the storm.

3 Thy bountiful care what tongue can recite?
It breathes in the air, it shines in the light,
It streams from the hills, it descends to the plain,
And sweetly distills in the dew and the rain.

4 Frail children of dust, and feeble as frail,
In thee do we trust, nor find thee to fail;

Thy mercies how tender! how firm to the end!
Our Maker, Defender, Redeemer, and Friend.
GRANT.

58.　　　*"A God doing Wonders."*　　C. M.

I SING th' almighty power of God,
　　That made the mountains rise,
That spread the flowing seas abroad,
　　And built the lofty skies.

2 I sing the goodness of the Lord,
　　That filled the earth with food;
He formed the creatures with his word,
　　And then pronounced them good.

3 Lord, how thy wonders are displayed,
　　Where'er I turn mine eye;
If I survey the ground I tread,
　　Or gaze upon the sky!

4 Creatures that borrow life from thee
　　Are subject to thy care;
There's not a place where we can flee,
　　But God is present there.　　WATTS.

59.　　　Psalm xciii.　　H. M.

THE Lord Jehovah reigns;
　　His throne is built on high;
The garments he assumes
　　Are light and majesty:
His glories shine with beams so bright,
No mortal eye can bear the sight.

2 The thunders of his hand
　　Keep the wide world in awe;
His wrath and justice stand
　　To guard his holy law;

And where his love resolves to bless,
His truth confirms and seals the grace.

> 3 And can this mighty King
> Of glory condescend?
> And will he write his name,
> "My Father and my Friend?"
> I love his name; I love his word:
> Join, all my powers, and praise the Lord!

WATTS.

60.   *God in Nature.*   L. M. 61.

THOU art, O God, the life and light
Of all this wondrous world we see;
Its glow by day, its smile by night,
Are but reflections caught from thee:
Where'er we turn, thy glories shine,
And all things fair and bright are thine.

2 When youthful spring around us breathes,
Thy spirit warms her fragrant sigh;
And every flower the summer wreathes
Is born beneath thy kindling eye:
Where'er we turn, thy glories shine,
And all things fair and bright are thine.

MOORE.

61.   *God in Nature.*   L. M.

THERE'S nothing bright above, below,
From flowers that bloom to stars that glow,
But in its light my soul can see
Some features of the Deity.

2 There's nothing dark below, above,
But in its gloom I trace Thy love,
And meekly wait the moment when
Thy touch shall make all bright again.

3 The light, the dark, where'er I look,
Shall be one pure and shining book,
Where I may read, in words of flame,
The glories of Thy wondrous name.   MOORE.

62.   *The Creator's Works.*   C. M.

THERE'S not a star whose twinkling light
   Illumes the distant earth,
And cheers the solemn gloom of night,
   But mercy gave it birth.

2 There's not a cloud whose dews distill
   Upon the parching clod,
And clothe with verdure vale and hill,
   That is not sent by God.

3 There's not a place in earth's vast round,
   In ocean deep, or air,
Where skill and wisdom are not found,
   For God is everywhere.

4 Around, beneath, below, above,
   Wherever space extends,
There heaven displays its boundless love,
   And power with mercy blends.

63.   *Power and Goodness of God.*   C. M.

'TIS by thy strength the mountains stand,
   God of eternal power!
The sea grows calm at thy command,
   And tempests cease to roar.

2 Thy morning light and evening shade
   Successive comforts bring;
Thy plenteous fruits make harvest glad,
   Thy flowers adorn the spring.

3 Seasons and times and moons and hours,
　　Heaven, earth, and air are thine;
When clouds distill in fruitful showers,
　　The author is divine!

4 Thy showers the thirsty furrows fill,
　　And ranks of corn appear;
Thy ways abound with blessings still,
　　Thy goodness crowns the year.　　WATTS.

64.　　　*The All-seeing God.*　　L. M.

LORD, thou hast searched and seen me through;
Thine eye commands, with piercing view,
My rising and my resting hours,
My heart and flesh, with all their powers.

2 My thoughts, before they are my own,
Are to my God distinctly known;
He knows the words I mean to speak,
Ere from my opening lips they break.

3 Within thy circling power I stand;
On every side I find thy hand;
Awake, asleep, at home, abroad,
I am surrounded still with God.

4 Oh, may these thoughts possess my breast,
Where'er I rove, where'er I rest!
Nor let my weaker passions dare
Consent to sin, for God is there.　　WATTS.

65.　　　*God present Everywhere.*　　S. M.

GOD of almighty power,
　　How glorious are thy ways!
Angels thy majesty adore,
　　All creatures speak thy praise.

2 Wherever earth is fair,
  Or brighter worlds extend,
Almighty Sovereign! thou art there,
  Creation's Lord and Friend.

3 And where the stars are not,
  Nor sun hath ever shone,
Beyond the flight of human thought,
  There thou art God alone.

66.   *"Thrice Holy Lord."*   C. M.

HOLY and reverend is the name
  Of our eternal King:
"Thrice holy Lord!" the angels cry;
  "Thrice holy!" let us sing.

2 The deepest reverence of the mind,
  Pay, O my soul! to God;
Lift, with thy hands, a holy heart,
  To his sublime abode.

3 With sacred awe pronounce his name,
  Whom words nor thoughts can reach;
A broken heart shall please him more
  Than noblest forms of speech.

4 Thou holy God! preserve my soul
  From all pollution free;
The pure in heart are thy delight,
  And they thy face shall see.
                         NEEDHAM.

67.   *Mercies of God:*   S. M.

MY soul, repeat his praise,
  Whose mercies are so great;
Whose anger is so slow to rise,
  So ready to abate.

GOODNESS OF GOD. 41

2 His power subdues our sins,
    And his forgiving love,
Far as the east is from the west,
    Doth all our guilt remove.

3 High as the heavens are raised
    Above the ground we tread,
So far the riches of his grace
    Our highest thoughts exceed.
                        WATTS.

68.   *Divine Goodness.*   L. M.

TRIUMPHANT Lord, thy goodness reigns
    Through all the wide celestial plains;
And its full streams unceasing flow
    Down to the abodes of men below.

2 Through nature's work its glories shine;
    The cares of providence are thine;
And grace erects our ruined frame
    A fairer temple to thy name.

3 Oh, give to every human heart
    To taste and feel how good thou art;
With grateful love and reverent fear,
    To know how blest thy children are.
                        DODDRIDGE.

69.   *Divine Goodness.*   C. M.

THY goodness, Lord, our souls confess;
    Thy goodness we adore;
A spring whose blessings never fail,
    A sea without a shore.

2 Sun, moon, and stars thy love attest
    In every golden ray;
Love draws the curtain of the night
    And love brings back the day.

3 Thy bounty every season crowns
  With all the bliss it yields;
With joyful clusters loads the vines,
  With strengthening grain the fields.

4 But chiefly thy compassion, Lord,
  Is in the gospel seen;
There, like a sun, thy mercy shines,
  Without a cloud between.   GIBBONS.

70. *The Divine Compassion.* S. M.

THE pity of the Lord
  To those that fear his name
Is such as tender parents feel;
  He knows our feeble frame.

2 He knows we are but dust,
  Scattered with every breath;
His anger, like a rising wind,
  Can send us swift to death.

3 Our days are as the grass,
  Or like the morning flower;
When blasting winds sweep o'er the field,
  It withers in an hour.

4 But thy compassions, Lord,
  To endless years endure;
And children's children ever find
  Thy words of promise sure.   WATTS.

71. *Source of Good.* C. P. M.

GREAT Source of unexhausted good!
  Who giv'st us help, and friends, and food,
    And peace, and calm content;
Like fragrant incense to the skies,

Let songs of grateful praises rise,
  For all thy blessings lent.

2 Through all the dangers of the day,
Thy providence attends our way,
  To guard us and to guide;
Thy grace directs our wandering will,
And warns us, lest seducing ill
  Allure our souls aside.

3 To thee our lives, our all we owe,
Our peace and sweetest joys below,
  And brighter hopes above;
Then let our lives, and all that's ours,
Our souls and all our active powers,
  Be sacred to thy love.

4 Thus, gracious Father! thee we praise;
And while our feeble songs we raise
  To bless thee and adore,
Some spark of heavenly fire impart,
And teach each humble, grateful heart
  To bless and love thee more.

72.   1 Peter v. 7.   S. M.

HOW gentle God's commands!
  How kind his precepts are!
Come, cast your burdens on the Lord,
  And trust his constant care.

2 Beneath his watchful eye
  His saints securely dwell;
That Hand which bears creation up,
  Shall guard his children well.

3 Why should this anxious load
  Press down your weary mind?
Haste to your heavenly Father's throne,
  And sweet refreshment find.

4 His goodness stands approved,
  Unchanged from day to day:
I'll drop my burden at his feet,
  And bear a song away.   DODDRIDGE.

73.   *God our Benefactor.*   S. M.

MY Maker and my King!
  To thee my all I owe;
Thy sovereign bounty is the spring
  Whence all my blessings flow.

2 The creature of thy hand,
  On thee alone I live;
My God! thy benefits demand
  More praise than I can give.

3 Lord, what can I impart,
  When all is thine before?
Thy love demands a thankful heart;
  The gift, alas, how poor!

4 Shall I withhold thy due?
  And shall my passions rove?
Lord, form this wretched heart anew
  And fill it with thy love.
                    MRS. STEELE.

74.   *Remembrance of Divine Mercies.*   C. M.

WHEN all thy mercies, O my God,
  My rising soul surveys,
Transported with the view, I'm lost
  In wonder, love, and praise!

2 Ten thousand, thousand precious gifts
  My daily thanks employ;
Nor is the least a cheerful heart,
  That tastes those gifts with joy.

3 Through every period of my life
   Thy goodness I'll pursue;
And after death, in distant worlds,
   The glorious theme renew. ADDISON.

75.   *Benevolence of God's Decrees.* C. M.

SINCE all the varying scenes of time
   God's watchful eye surveys,
Oh, who so wise to choose our lot,
   Or to appoint our ways!

2 Good when he gives, supremely good;
   Nor less when he denies;
Ev'n crosses from his sovereign hand,
   Are blessings in disguise.

3 Why should we doubt a Father's love,
   So constant and so kind?
To his unerring, gracious will
   Be every wish resigned. HERVEY.

76.   *Confidence in God.* 7s. & 6s.

IN heavenly love abiding,
   No change my heart shall fear,
And safe is such confiding,
   For nothing changes here:
The storm may roar without me,
   My heart may low be laid,
But God is round about me,
   And can I be dismayed?

2 Wherever he may guide me,
   No want shall turn me back;
My Shepherd is beside me,
   And nothing can I lack:
His wisdom ever waketh,
   His sight is never dim;

  He knows the way he taketh,
   And I will walk with him.

 3 Green pastures are before me,
   Which yet I have not seen;
 Bright skies will soon be o'er me,
   Where darkest clouds have been:
 My hope I can not measure;
   My path to life is free;
 My Saviour has my treasure,
   And he will walk with me.
WARING.

77.   *God's Mercies Innumerable.* L. M.

THIS curious frame, these noble powers,
 To thy creating hand I owe:
Thy providence preserves me safe,
 And crowns my every wish below.

2 The various and exhaustless theme
 Each rising morn my soul pursues,
In fervent prayer ascends to thee,
 And still her grateful song renews.

3 Thy mercies, Lord, through endless years,
 Shall still my raptured powers employ;
Yet endless years will still but swell
 My wonder, gratitude, and joy.
E. SCOTT.

78.   *God is Love.* C. P. M.

MY God! thy boundless love I praise;
 How bright on high its glories blaze!
  How sweetly bloom below!
It streams from thine eternal throne;
Through heaven its joys forever run,
  And o'er the earth they flow.

2 'Tis love that paints the purple morn,
And bids the clouds, in air upborne,
   Their genial drops distill;
In every vernal beam it glows,
And breathes in every gale that blows,
   And glides in every rill.

3 It robes in cheerful green the ground,
And pours its flowery beauties round,
   Whose sweets perfume the gale;
Its bounties richly spread the plain,
The blushing fruit, the golden grain,
   And smile in every vale.

4 Then let the love, that makes me blest,
With cheerful praise inspire my breast,
   And ardent gratitude;
And all my thoughts and passions tend
To thee, my Father and my Friend,
   My soul's eternal good.   H. MORE.

79.   *God is Love.*   8s. & 7s.

GOD is love; his mercy brightens
   All the path in which we rove;
Bliss he wakes, and woe he lightens:
   God is wisdom, God is love.

2 Chance and change are busy ever;
   Man decays, and ages move:
But his mercy waneth never;
   God is wisdom, God is love.

3 Ev'n the hour that darkest seemeth
   Will his changeless goodness prove;
From the gloom his brightness streameth:
   God is wisdom, God is love.

4 He with earthly cares entwineth
    Hope and comfort from above:
Everywhere his glory shineth;
    God is wisdom, God is love.
                              BOWRING.

80.   *Love.*—1 John iv. 8.   C. M.

COME, ye that know and fear the Lord,
    And raise your thoughts above:
Let every heart and voice accord,
    To sing that "God is love."

2 This precious truth his word declares,
    And all his mercies prove;
Jesus, the gift of gifts, appears,
    To show that "God is love."

3 Behold his patience, bearing long
    With those who from him rove;
Till mighty grace their hearts subdues,
    To teach them—"God is love."

4 Oh, may we all, while here below,
    This best of blessings prove;
Till warmer hearts, in brighter worlds,
    Proclaim that "God is love."   BURDER.

81.   *God is Good.*   C. M.

I BOW my forehead to the dust,
    I veil my eyes for shame,
And urge, in trembling self-distrust,
    A prayer without a claim.

2 I see the wrong that round me lies,
    I feel the guilt within,
I hear with groans and travail-cries
    The world confess its sin.

3 Yet in the maddening maze of things,
　　And tossed by storm and flood,
To one fixed star my spirit clings—
　　I know that God is good!

4 I know not where his islands lift
　　Their fronted palms in air;
I only know I can not drift
　　Beyond his love and care.

5 And so beside the silent sea
　　I wait the muffled oar;
No harm from him can come to me,
　　On ocean or on shore!　　　WHITTIER.

82.　　　*Love.*—Ephesians iii. 17-19.　　H. M.

OH, for a shout of joy,
　　Worthy the theme we sing;
To this divine employ
　　Our hearts and voices bring;
Sound, sound, thro' all the earth abroad,
The love, th' eternal love of God.

2 Unnumbered myriads stand,
　　Of seraphs bright and fair,
Or bow at thy right hand,
　　And pay their homage there;
But strive in vain with loudest chord,
To sound thy wondrous love, O Lord.

3 Though earth and hell assail,
　　And doubts and fears arise,
The weakest shall prevail,
　　And grasp the heavenly prize,
And through an endless age record
Thy love, thy changeless love, O Lord.
　　　　　　　　　　　　YOUNG.

D

83. *Love of God.* L. M. 6l.

THOU hidden Love of God, whose height,
  Whose depth unfathomed, no man knows,
I see from far thy beauteous light;
  Inly I sigh for thy repose:
My heart is pained, nor can it be
At rest till it finds rest in thee!

2 Is there a thing beneath the sun
  That strives with me my heart to share?
Ah! tear it thence, and reign alone,
  The Lord of every motion there:
Then shall my heart from earth be free,
When it has found repose in thee!
                              C. WESLEY.

84. *"His compassions fail not."* 8s. 7s. & 4s.

EVERY human tie may perish;
  Friend to friend unfaithful prove;
Mothers cease their own to cherish;
  Heaven and earth at last remove:
    But no changes
Can avert the Father's love.

2 In the furnace God may prove thee,
  Thence to bring thee forth more bright,
But can never cease to love thee;
  Thou art precious in his sight:
    God is with thee;
God, thine everlasting Light.   KELLY.

85. *Dependence upon God.* C. M.

O LORD, I would delight in thee,
  And on thy care depend;
To thee in every trouble flee,
  My best, my only Friend.

2 When all created streams are dried,
  Thy fullness is the same:
May I with this be satisfied,
  And glory in thy name!

3 No good in creatures can be found,
  But what is found in thee;
I must have all things and abound
  While God is God to me.

4 O Lord, I cast my care on thee,
  I triumph and adore:
Henceforth my great concern shall be
  To love and please thee more.
                              RYLAND.

86.   *The Almighty Refuge.*   L. M.

UP to the hills I lift mine eyes,
  Th' eternal hills beyond the skies;
Thence all her help my soul derives,
There my almighty Refuge lives.

2 He lives—the everlasting God
That built the world, that spread the flood:
The heavens with all their hosts he made,
And the dark regions of the dead.

3 He guides our feet, he guards our way;
His morning smiles bless all the day:
He spreads the evening veil, and keeps
The silent hours, while Israel sleeps.
                              WATTS.

87.   Psalm cxxi.   C. M.

TO heaven I lift my waiting eyes,
  There all my hopes are laid:
The Lord that built the earth and skies
  Is my perpetual aid.

2 Their steadfast feet shall never fall
      Whom he designs to keep:
  His ear attends the softest call,
      His eyes can never sleep.

  3 He guards thy soul, he keeps thy breath,
      Where thickest dangers come;
  Go and return, secure from death,
      Till God commands thee home. WATTS.

88.   *Looking up.*   H. M.

  UPWARD I lift mine eyes,
      From God is all my aid;
  The God who built the skies,
      And earth and nature made:
  God is the tower | His grace is nigh
  To which I fly; | In every hour.

  2 No burning heats by day,
      Nor blasts of evening air,
  Shall take my health away,
      If God be with me there:
  Thou art my sun, | To guard my head
  And thou my shade, | By night or noon.

  3 Hast thou not given thy word
      To save my soul from death?
  And I can trust my Lord
      To keep my mortal breath:
  I'll go and come, | Till from on high
  Nor fear to die, | Thou call me home.
                                WATTS.

89.   Psalm xci.   8s. & 7s.

  CALL Jehovah thy salvation,
      Rest beneath th' Almighty's shade;

In his secret habitation
  Dwell, and never be dismayed!

2 There no tumult can alarm thee,
  Thou shalt dread no hidden snare;
Guile nor violence can harm thee,
  In eternal safeguard there.

3 He shall charge his angel legions
  Watch and ward o'er thee to keep,
Though thou walk through hostile regions,
  Though in desert wilds thou sleep.

4 Since with firm and pure affection
  Thou on God hast set thy love,
With the wings of his protection
  He shall shield thee from above.

5 Thou shalt call on him in trouble,
  He will hearken, he will save;
Here for grief reward thee double,
  Crown with life beyond the grave.
                MONTGOMERY.

90. *Trust in God.*   7s. & 6s.

GOD is my strong salvation;
  What foe have I to fear?
In darkness and temptation,
  My Light, my Help is near.

2 Though hosts encamp around me,
  Firm in the fight I stand;
What terror can confound me,
  With God at my right hand?

3 Place on the Lord reliance;
  My soul, with courage wait;
His truth be thine affiance
  When faint and desolate.

4 His might thy heart shall strengthen,
  His love thy joy increase;
Mercy thy days shall lengthen;
  The Lord will give thee peace.
                    MONTGOMERY.

91.   *Joy in the Presence of God.*   8s. 7s. & 4s.

THOU, O Lord, wilt never leave me,
  Thou wilt never me forsake;
Thou wilt keep and thou wilt save me,
  While thy word my guide I make:
    Save from evil
  For thy name and mercy's sake!

2 When my soul is dark and clouded,
  Torn with doubt and worn with care,
Through the vail by which 'tis shrouded,
  Light from heaven will soon appear;
    And thy presence
  Banish every doubt and fear.

3 When my sky above is glowing,
  And around me all is bright;
Pleasure, like a river flowing,
  Fills my soul with sweet delight:
    Thou wilt keep me,
  Thou wilt guide my steps aright.

92.   *Unchanging Trust.*   C. M.

NO change of time shall ever shock
  My trust, O Lord, in thee;
For thou hast always been my Rock,
  A sure defense to me.

2 Thou my deliverer art, O God;
  My trust is in thy power:

Thou art my shield from foes abroad,
  My safeguard and my tower.

3 To thee will I address my prayer,
  To whom all praise I owe;
So shall I by thy watchful care
  Be saved from every foe.

93.   *Divine Guidance.*   L. M.

"HE leadeth me!" Oh, blessed thought,
Oh, words with heavenly comfort fraught,
Whate'er I do, where'er I be,
Still 'tis God's hand that leadeth me!

2 Sometimes 'mid scenes of deepest gloom,
Sometimes where Eden's bowers bloom,
By waters still, o'er troubled sea—
Still 'tis his hand that leadeth me!

3 Lord, I would clasp thy hand in mine,
Nor ever murmur nor repine—
Content, whatever lot I see,
Since 'tis my God that leadeth me.

4 And when my task on earth is done,
When, by thy grace, the victory's won,
E'en death's cold wave I will not flee,
Since God through Jordan leadeth me.

94.   *Divine Protection.*   7s.

THEY who on the Lord rely
  Safely dwell, though danger's nigh;
Lo, his sheltering wings are spread
O'er each faithful servant's head.

2 Vain temptation's wily snare:
They shall be the Father's care;

Harmless flies the shaft by day,
Or in darkness wings its way.

3 When they wake or when they sleep,
Angel guards their vigils keep;
Death and danger may be near,
Faith and love can never fear.

95.   *Rest in God.*   S. M.

OH, cease, my wandering soul,
  On restless wing to roam;
All this wide world, to either pole,
  Hath not for thee a home.

2 Behold the ark of God!
  Behold the open door!
Oh, haste to gain that dear abode,
  And rove, my soul, no more.

3 There safe thou shalt abide,
  There sweet shall be thy rest,
And every longing satisfied,
  With full salvation blest.

MUHLENBERG.

96.   *Security.*   S. M.

I STAND on Zion's mount,
  And view my starry crown;
No power on earth my hope can shake,
  Nor hell can thrust me down.

2 The lofty hills and towers,
  That lift their heads on high,
Shall all be leveled low in dust—
  Their very names shall die.

3 The vaulted heavens shall fall,
  Built by Jehovah's hands;

But, firmer than the heavens, the Rock
  Of my salvation stands.   SWAIN.

97.   *Trust in God.*   S. M.

WHERE wilt thou put thy trust?
  In a frail form of clay,
That to its element of dust
  Must soon resolve away?

2 Where wilt thou cast thy care?
  Upon an erring heart,
Which hath its own sore ills to bear,
  And shrinks from sorrow's dart?

3 No—place thy trust above
  This shadowy realm of night,
In Him whose boundless power and love
  Thy confidence invite.

4 His mercies still endure
  When skies and stars grow dim;
His changeless promise standeth sure,
  Go—cast thy care on him.
                SIGOURNEY.

98.   *Paternal Care.*   7s. D.

FATHER! thy paternal care
  Has my guardian been, my guide;
Every hallowed wish and prayer
  Has thy hand of love supplied:
Thine is every thought of bliss
  Left by hours and days gone by;
Every hope thy offering is,
  Beaming from futurity.

2 Every sun of splendid ray,
  Every moon that shines serene,

Every morn that welcomes day,
　Every evening's twilight scene,
Every hour which wisdom brings,
　Every incense at thy shrine—
These, and all life's holiest things,
　And its fairest—all are thine.

3 And for all, my hymns shall rise
　Daily to thy gracious throne:
Thither let my asking eyes
　Turn unwearied, righteous One!
Through life's strange vicissitude,
　There reposing all my care;
Trusting still, through ill and good,
　Fixed, and cheered, and counseled there.
　　　　　　　　　　　BOWRING.

99. *"Whom have I in heaven but Thee?"* 7s. D.

LORD of earth! thy forming hand
　Well this beauteous frame hath planned,
Woods that wave, and hills that tower,
Ocean rolling in his power:
Yet, amid this scene so fair,
Should I cease thy smile to share,
What were all its joys to me?
Whom have I on earth but thee?

2 Lord of heaven! beyond our sight
Shines a world of purer light:
There, in love's unclouded reign,
Parted hands shall meet again:
Oh, that world is passing fair!
Yet, if thou wert absent there,
What were all its joys to me?
Whom have I in heaven but thee?　GRANT.

TRUST IN GOD.

100. Psalm lxxiii. 25. C. M.

WHOM have we, Lord, in heaven, but thee,
  And whom on earth beside?
Where else for succor can we flee,
  Or in whose strength confide?

2 Thou art our portion here below,
  Our promised bliss above;
Ne'er may our souls an object know
  So precious as thy love.

3 When heart and flesh, O Lord, shall fail,
  Thou wilt our spirit cheer,
Support us through life's thorny vale,
  And calm each anxious fear.

4 Yes, thou shalt be our guide through life,
  And help and strength supply,
Sustain us in death's fearful strife,
  And welcome us on high. LYTE.

101. *All vain, without God's Blessing.* 8s. & 7s.

VAINLY through night's weary hours
  Keep we watch lest foes alarm;
Vain our bulwarks and our towers,
  But for God's protecting arm.

2 Vain were all our toil and labor,
  Did not God that labor bless;
Vain, without his grace and favor,
  Every talent we possess.

3 Vainer still the hope of heaven
  That on human strength relies;
But to him shall help be given
  Who in humble faith applies.
          LYTE.

HOLY SCRIPTURES.

102. *The Bible for the Young.* C. M.

How shall the young secure their hearts,
  And guard their lives from sin?
Thy word the choicest rules imparts,
  To keep the conscience clean.

2 'Tis like the sun, a heavenly light,
  That guides us all the day;
And, through the dangers of the night,
  A lamp to lead our way.

3 Thy word is everlasting truth;
  How pure is every page!
Thy holy book shall guide our youth,
  And well support our age.   WATTS.

103. *The Bible the Light of the World.* C. M.

A glory gilds the sacred page,
  Majestic, like the sun;
It gives a light to every age;
  It gives, but borrows none.

2 The hand that gave it still supplies
  The gracious light and heat:
Its truths upon the nations rise;
  They rise, but never set.

3 Let everlasting thanks be thine
  For such a bright display
As makes a world of darkness shine
  With beams of heavenly day.

4 My soul rejoices to pursue
   The steps of Him I love,
Till glory breaks upon my view
   In brighter worlds above!   COWPER.

104.   Psalm cxix.   C. M.

HOW precious is the book divine,
   By inspiration given!
Bright as a lamp its doctrines shine,
   To guide our souls to heaven.

2 It sweetly cheers our drooping hearts,
   In this dark vale of tears;
Life, light, and joy it still imparts,
   And quells our rising fears.

3 This lamp, through all the tedious night
   Of life, shall guide our way,
Till we behold the clearer light
   Of an eternal day.   FAWCETT.

105.   *Delight in the Scriptures.*   C. M.

FATHER of mercies, in thy word
   What endless glory shines!
Forever be thy name adored
   For these celestial lines.

2 Here my Redeemer's welcome voice
   Spreads heavenly peace around;
And life and everlasting joys
   Attend the blissful sound.

3 Oh, may these heavenly pages be
   My ever dear delight;
And still new beauties may I see,
   And still increasing light!

4 Divine Instructor, gracious Lord,
   Be thou forever near;
Teach me to love thy sacred word,
   And view my Saviour there.
Mrs. Steele.

106.   Psalm cxix. 105.   C. M.

LAMP of our feet! whereby we trace
   Our path when wont to stray;
Stream from the fount of heavenly grace!
   Brook by the traveller's way!

2 Bread of our souls! whereon we feed;
   True manna from on high!
Our guide and chart! wherein we read
   Of realms beyond the sky.

3 Pillar of fire through watches dark,
   And radiant cloud by day!
When waves would whelm our tossing bark,
   Our anchor and our stay!

4 Word of the everlasting God!
   Will of his glorious Son!
Without thee how could earth be trod,
   Or heaven itself be won?

5 Lord, grant us all aright to learn
   The wisdom it imparts,
And to its heavenly teaching turn
   With simple, child-like hearts.
Barton.

JESUS CHRIST.

107. *Birth of Christ.* 8s. & 7s.

HARK! what mean those holy voices,
  Sweetly sounding through the skies?
Lo! th' angelic host rejoices;
  Heavenly hallelujahs rise.

2 Hear them tell the wondrous story,
  Hear them chant in hymns of joy—
"Glory in the highest, glory!
  Glory be to God most high!

3 "Peace on earth, good-will from heaven,
  Reaching far as man is found;
Souls redeemed, and sins forgiven!
  Loud our golden harps shall sound.

4 "Christ is born, the great Anointed;
  Heaven and earth his praises sing!
Oh, receive whom God appointed,
  For your Prophet, Priest, and King!

5 "Haste, ye mortals, to adore him;
  Learn his name, and taste his joy;
Till in heaven ye sing before him—
  'Glory be to God most high!'"

CAWOOD.

108. *The Star in the East.* 11s. & 10s.

BRIGHTEST and best of the sons of the morning!
  Dawn on our darkness, and lend us thine aid;
Star of the East, the horizon adorning,
  Guide where our infant Redeemer is laid.

2 Say, shall we yield him, in costly devotion,
  Odors of Edom, and off'rings divine?
Gems of the mountain, and pearls of the ocean,
  Myrrh from the forest, or gold from the mine?

3 Vainly we offer each ample oblation,
  Vainly with gold would his favors secure:
Richer, by far, is the heart's adoration;
  Dearer to God are the prayers of the poor.

4 Brightest and best of the sons of the morning!
  Dawn on our darkness, and lend us thine aid;
Star of the East, the horizon adorning,
  Guide where our infant Redeemer is laid.
HEBER.

109. *"On earth peace."*—Luke ii. C. M.

CALM, on the listening ear of night,
  Come heaven's melodious strains,
Where wild Judea stretches far
  Her silver-mantled plains.

2 Celestial choirs, from courts above,
  'Mid sacred glories there;
And angels, with their sparkling lyres,
  Make music on the air.

3 The answering hills of Palestine
  Send back the glad reply;
And greet, from all their holy heights,
  The day-spring from on high.

4 O'er the blue depths of Galilee
  There comes a holier calm;
And Sharon waves, in solemn praise,
  Her silent groves of palm.

5 Light on thy hills, Jerusalem!
  The Saviour now is born!

And bright on Bethlehem's joyous plains
Breaks the first Christmas morn.
E. H. SEARS.

110. *Christ our Example.* L. M.

MY dear Redeemer and my Lord,
I read my duty in thy word;
But in thy life the law appears,
Drawn out in living characters.

2 Such was thy truth, and such thy zeal,
Such deference to thy Father's will,
Such love and meekness so divine,
I would transcribe and make them mine.

3 Cold mountains and the midnight air
Witnessed the fervor of thy prayer:
The desert thy temptations knew,
Thy conflict and thy victory too.

4 Be thou my pattern: make me bear
More of thy gracious image here:
Then God, the Judge, shall own my name
Among the followers of the Lamb.
WATTS.

111. *Christ our Example.* L. M.

MAKE us, by thy transforming grace,
Dear Saviour, daily more like thee!
Thy fair example may we trace,
To teach us what we ought to be!

2 To do thy heavenly Father's will
Was thy employment and delight;
Humility and holy zeal
Shone through thy life divinely bright.

3 But ah! how blind! how weak we are!
　　How frail! how apt to turn aside!
Lord, we depend upon thy care,
　　And ask thy Spirit for our guide.
　　　　　　　　　　　　Mrs. Steele.

112.   *All virtues seen in Christ.*   C. M.

BEHOLD, where, in a mortal form,
　　Appears each grace divine;
The virtues, all in Jesus met,
　　With mildest radiance shine.

2 'Mid keen reproach, and cruel scorn,
　　Patient and meek he stood:
His foes, ungrateful, sought his life;
　　He labored for their good.

3 In the last hour of deep distress,
　　Before his Father's throne,
With soul resigned, he bowed, and said,
　　"Thy will, not mine, be done!"

4 Be Christ our pattern and our guide;
　　His image may we bear:
Oh, may we tread his holy steps,
　　His joy and glory share!　　Enfield.

113.   Matt. xi. 28.   L. M.

HOW sweetly flowed the gospel sound
　　From lips of gentleness and grace,
When listening thousands gathered round,
　　And joy and gladness filled the place!

2 From heaven he came, of heaven he spoke,
　　To heaven he led his followers' way;
Dark clouds of gloomy night he broke,
　　Unvailing an immortal day.

3 "Come, wanderers, to my Father's home,
   Come, all ye weary ones, and rest:"
Yes, sacred Teacher, we will come,
   Obey thee, love thee, and be blest!
BOWRING.

114.   Cant. v. 10–16.   C. M.

MAJESTIC sweetness sits enthroned
   Upon the Saviour's brow;
His head with radiant glories crowned,
   His lips with grace o'erflow.

2 No mortal can with him compare,
   Among the sons of men:
Fairer is he than all the fair
   That fill the heavenly train.

3 To him I owe my life and breath,
   And all the joys I have;
He makes me triumph over death,
   He saves me from the grave.

4 Since from his bounty I receive
   Such proofs of love divine,
Had I a thousand hearts to give,
   Lord! they should all be thine.
STENNETT.

115.   1 Peter ii. 7.   C. M.

HOW sweet the name of Jesus sounds
   In a believer's ear!
It soothes his sorrows, heals his wounds,
   And drives away his fear.

2 It makes the wounded spirit whole,
   And calms the troubled breast;
'Tis manna to the hungry soul,
   And to the weary, rest.

3 Weak is the effort of my heart,
  And cold my warmest thought;
But when I see thee as thou art,
  I'll praise thee as I ought.

4 Till then I would thy love proclaim
  With every fleeting breath;
And may the music of thy name
  Refresh my soul in death.   NEWTON.

116.   *The New Song.*   S. M.

AWAKE, and sing the song
  Of Moses and the Lamb!
Wake every heart, and every tongue,
  To praise the Saviour's name!

2 Sing, till we feel our hearts
  Ascending with our tongues;
Sing, till the love of sin departs,
  And grace inspires our songs.

3 Soon shall we hear him say,
  "Ye blessed children, come!"
Soon will he call us hence away
  To our eternal home.

4 Soon shall our raptured tongue
  His endless praise proclaim,
And sweeter voices tune the song
  Of Moses and the Lamb.
              HAMMOND.

117.   Rom. v. 8.   C. M.

TO our Redeemer's glorious name
  Awake the sacred song!
Oh! may his love—immortal flame—
  Tune every heart and tongue!

2 His love, what mortal thought can reach?
   What mortal tongue display?
Imagination's utmost stretch,
   In wonder, dies away.

3 Dear Lord! while we adoring pay
   Our humble thanks to thee,
May every heart with rapture say,
   "The Saviour died for me!"
                               Mrs. Steele.

118.   *Loving-kindness.*   L. M.

AWAKE, my soul, to joyful lays,
And sing the great Redeemer's praise;
He justly claims a song from me:
His loving-kindness, oh, how free!

2 He saw me ruined in the fall,
Yet loved me, notwithstanding all;
He saved me from my lost estate:
His loving-kindness, oh, how great!

3 When trouble, like a gloomy cloud,
Has gathered thick and thundered loud,
He near my soul hath always stood:
His loving-kindness, oh, how good!

4 Soon shall I pass the gloomy vale;
Soon all my mortal powers must fail:
Oh, may my last expiring breath
His loving-kindness sing in death!
                               Medley.

119.   Proverbs xviii. 24.   8s. & 7s.

ONE there is, above all others,
   Well deserves the name of Friend;

His is love beyond a brother's,
  Costly, free, and knows no end.

2 When he lived on earth abased,
  Friend of sinners was his name;
Now above all glory raised,
  He rejoices in the same.

3 Oh! for grace our hearts to soften!
  Teach us, Lord, at length to love;
We, alas! forget too often
  What a Friend we have above.
                NEWTON.

120.   Rev. v. 12.   6s. & 4s.

GLORY to God on high!
  Let heaven and earth reply,
    "Praise ye his name!"
His love and grace adore,
Who all our sorrows bore;
Sing loud forevermore,
  "Worthy the Lamb!"

2 Join, all ye ransomed race,
Our Lord and God to bless:
  Praise ye his name!
In him we will rejoice,
And make a joyful noise,
Shouting with heart and voice,
  "Worthy the Lamb!"

3 Soon must we change our place,
Yet we will never cease
  Praising his name:
To him our songs we bring;
Hail him our glorious King;
And through all ages sing,
  "Worthy the Lamb!"

121. *Riches of Grace.* 7s.

JOYFUL be the hours to-day;
  Joyful let the seasons be;
Let us sing, for well we may:
  Jesus! we will sing of thee.

2 Joyful are we now to own,
  Rapture thrills us as we trace
All the deeds thy love hath done,
  All the riches of thy grace.

3 'Tis thy grace alone can save;
  Every blessing comes from thee—
All we have, and hope to have,
  All we are, and hope to be. KELLY.

122. *" Elect, precious."* C. M.

JESUS! I love thy charming name;
  'Tis music to mine ear:
Fain would I sound it out so loud
  That earth and heaven should hear.

2 All that my loftiest powers can wish,
  In thee doth richly meet;
Not to mine eyes is light so dear,
  Nor friendship half so sweet.

3 Thy grace still dwells upon my heart,
  And sheds its fragrance there—
The noblest balm of all my wounds,
  The cordial of my care. DODDRIDGE.

123. *Sympathy of Christ.* C. M.

WITH joy we meditate the grace
  Of our High Priest above:

His heart is made of tenderness—
It melts with pitying love.

2 Touched with a sympathy within,
He knows our feeble frame;
He knows what sore temptations mean,
For he hath felt the same.

3 Then let our humble faith address
His mercy and his power;
We shall obtain delivering grace
In the distressing hour. WATTS.

124. Heb. xiii. 8. L. M.

SWEETER to Jesus, when on earth,
Than angels' praise, the prayers of men;
And still thou art the same, O Lord,
The same dear Christ that thou wert then.

2 We have no tears thou wilt not dry;
We have no wounds thou wilt not heal;
No sorrows pierce our human hearts,
That thou, dear Saviour, dost not feel.

3 Thy pity like the dew distills,
And thy compassion, like the light,
Our every morning overfills,
And crowns with stars our every night.

4 Let not the world's rude conflict drown
The charmed music of thy voice,
That calls all weary souls to rest,
And bids all mourning souls rejoice.
H. KIMBALL.

125. Isaiah xlv. 22. 6s. & 4s.

MY faith looks up to thee,
Thou Lamb of Calvary,

Saviour Divine!
Now hear me while I pray;
Take all my guilt away;
Oh, let me, from this day,
  Be wholly thine!

2 May thy rich grace impart
Strength to my fainting heart,
  My zeal inspire!
As thou hast died for me,
Oh, may my love to thee
Pure, warm, and changeless be—
  A living fire!

3 While life's dark maze I tread,
And griefs around me spread,
  Be thou my guide;
Bid darkness turn to day,
Wipe sorrow's tears away,
Nor let me ever stray
  From thee aside.

4 When ends life's transient dream,
When death's cold, sullen stream
  Shall o'er me roll,
Blest Saviour! then, in love,
Fear and distrust remove;
Oh, bear me safe above—
  A ransomed soul!   RAY PALMER.

126.   1 Peter ii. 7.   C. P. M.

OH, could I speak the matchless worth,
  Oh, could I sound the glories forth,
    Which in my Saviour shine!
I'd soar, and touch the heavenly strings,
And vie with Gabriel while he sings
    In notes almost divine.

2 I'd sing the characters he bears,
And all the forms of love he wears,
  Exalted on his throne:
In loftiest songs of sweetest praise,
I would to everlasting days
  Make all his glories known.

3 Well—the delightful day will come,
When my dear Lord will bring me home,
  And I shall see his face:
Then with my Saviour, Brother, Friend,
A blest eternity I'll spend,
  Triumphant in his grace.   MEDLEY.

127. *Praise to the Saviour.*   7s. & 6s.

TO thee, O blessed Saviour,
  My heart exulting sings,
Rejoicing in thy favor,
  Almighty King of kings!
I'll celebrate thy glory,
  With all thy saints above,
And tell the joyful story
  Of thy redeeming love.

2 Soon as the morn with roses
  Bedecks the dewy east,
And when the sun reposes
  Upon the ocean's breast,
My voice, in supplication,
  Well-pleased the Lord shall hear:
Oh! grant me thy salvation,
  And to my soul draw near.

3 By thee, through life supported,
  I'll pass the dangerous road,
With heavenly hosts escorted,
  Up to thy bright abode;

Then cast my crown before thee,
    And, all my conflicts o'er,
  Unceasingly adore thee:
    What could an angel more?
                              HAWEIS.

128.   John xiv. 6.   C. M.

THOU art the Way: to thee alone
    From sin and death we flee;
  And he who would the Father seek,
    Must seek him, Lord, by thee.

2 Thou art the Truth: thy word alone
    True wisdom can impart;
  Thou only canst instruct the mind,
    And purify the heart.

3 Thou art the Life: the rending tomb
    Proclaims thy conquering arm;
  And those who put their trust in thee
    Nor death nor hell shall harm.

4 Thou art the Way, the Truth, the Life:
    Grant us to know that Way;
  That Truth to keep, that Life to win,
    Which leads to endless day.   DOANE.

129.   *"I am the Light of the World."*   7s. 6l.

CHRIST, whose glory fills the skies,
    Christ, the true, the only light,
  Sun of Righteousness! arise:
    Triumph o'er the shades of night;
  Day-spring from on high, be near;
  Day-star, in my heart appear!

2 Dark and cheerless is the morn,
    If thy light is hid from me;

Joyless is the day's return,
　Till thy mercy's beams I see—
Till they inward light impart,
　Glad my eyes, and warm my heart.

3 Visit, then, this soul of mine:
　Pierce the gloom of sin and grief,
Fill me, radiant Sun divine!
　Scatter all my unbelief:
More and more thyself display,
Shining to the perfect day.　　Toplady.

130.　　　John vi. 51.　　　L. M.

AWAY from earth my spirit turns,
　Away from every transient good;
With strong desire my bosom burns,
　To feast on heaven's immortal food.

2 Thou, Saviour, art the living bread;
　Thou wilt my every want supply:
By thee sustained, and cheered, and led,
　I'll press through dangers to the sky.

3 What though temptations oft distress,
　And sin assails and breaks my peace;
Thou wilt uphold, and save, and bless,
　And bid the storms of passion cease.

4 Then let me take thy gracious hand,
　And walk beside thee onward still;
Till my glad feet shall safely stand
　Forever firm on Zion's hill.
　　　　　　　　　Ray Palmer.

131.　　*Redeeming Love.*　　8s. & 7s.

SAVIOUR, source of every blessing,
　Tune my heart to grateful lays;

Streams of mercy, never ceasing,
  Call for ceaseless songs of praise.
2 Teach me some melodious measure,
  Sung by raptured saints above;
Fill my soul with sacred pleasure,
  While I sing redeeming love.
3 By thy hand restored, defended,
  Safe through life, thus far, I'm come;
Safe, O Lord, when life is ended,
  Bring me to my heavenly home.
                              ROBINSON.

132.   Matt. xxviii. 20.   8s. & 7s.
ALWAYS with us, always with us—
  Words of cheer and words of love;
Thus the risen Saviour whispers
  From his dwelling-place above.
2 With us when we toil in sadness,
  Sowing much and reaping none;
Telling us that in the future
  Golden harvests shall be won.
3 With us when the storm is sweeping
  O'er our pathway dark and drear;
Waking hope within our bosoms,
  Stilling every anxious fear.
4 With us in the lonely valley,
  When we cross the chilling stream!
Lighting up the steps to glory
  With salvation's radiant beam.   NEVIN.

133.   *The Shelter of the Cross.*   C. M.
OPPRESSED with noonday's scorching heat,
  To yonder Cross I flee;

Beneath its shelter take my seat:
  No shade like this for me!

2 Beneath that Cross clear waters burst—
  A fountain sparkling free;
And there I quench my desert thirst:
  No spring like this for me!

3 A stranger here, I pitch my tent
  Beneath this spreading tree;
Here shall my pilgrim life be spent:
  No home like this for me!

4 For burdened ones a resting-place,
  Beside that Cross I see;
I here cast off my weariness:
  No rest like this for me! BONAR.

134.   *Bearing the Cross.*   C. M.

LORD, as to thy dear cross we flee,
  And pray to be forgiven,
So let thy life our pattern be,
  And form our souls for heaven.

2 Help us, through good report and ill,
  Our daily cross to bear;
Like thee, to do our Father's will,
  Our brother's griefs to share.

3 Let grace our selfishness expel,
  Our earthliness refine;
And kindness in our bosoms dwell
  As free and true as thine.

4 Kept peaceful in the midst of strife,
  Forgiving and forgiven,
Oh, may we lead the pilgrim's life,
  And follow thee to heaven!

135. *Rest in Christ.* 11s. & 10s.

COME unto me, when shadows darkly gather,
  When the sad heart is weary and distressed;
Seeking for comfort from your heavenly Father,
  "Come unto me, and I will give you rest."

2 Large are the mansions in our Father's dwelling,
  Glad are those homes that sorrows never dim;
Sweet are the harps in holy music swelling,
  Soft are the tones that raise the heavenly hymn.

3 There, like an Eden blossoming in gladness,
  Bloom the fair flowers by earth so rudely pressed;
Come unto him, all ye who droop in sadness.
  "Come unto me, and I will give you rest."

136. *"Come unto Me."* C. M. D.

I HEARD the voice of Jesus say,
  "Come unto me and rest;
Lay down, thou weary one, lay down
  Thy head upon my breast:"
I came to Jesus as I was,
  Weary, and worn, and sad;
I found in him a resting-place,
  And he has made me glad.

2 I heard the voice of Jesus say,
  "Behold, I freely give
The living water! thirsty one,
  Stoop down, and drink, and live."
I came to Jesus, and I drank
  Of that life-giving stream:
My thirst was quenched, my soul revived,
  And now I live in him.

3 I heard the voice of Jesus say,
  "I am this dark world's light:
Look unto me; thy morn shall rise,
  And all thy day be bright."
I looked to Jesus, and I found
  In him my Star, my Sun;
And in that light of life I'll walk
  Till all my journey's done.   BONAR.

137.   John xiv. 18.   11s.

COME, Jesus, Redeemer, abide thou with me;
  Come, gladden my spirit that waiteth for thee;
Thy smile every shadow shall chase from my heart,
And soothe every sorrow though keen be the smart.

2 Without thee but weakness, with thee I am strong;
By day thou shalt lead me, by night be my song;
Though dangers surround me, I still every fear,
Since thou, the Most Mighty, my Helper, art near.

3 Thy love, oh, how faithful! so tender, so pure!
Thy promise, faith's anchor, how steadfast and sure!
That love, like sweet sunshine, my cold heart can warm,
That promise make steady my soul in the storm.

4 Breathe, breathe on my spirit, oft ruffled, thy peace:
From restless, vain wishes, bid thou my heart cease;

In thee all its longings henceforward shall end,
Till, glad, to thy presence my soul shall ascend.
RAY PALMER.

138.   Hebrews xiii. 5.   11s.

HOW firm a foundation, ye saints of the Lord,
Is laid for your faith in his excellent word!
What more can he say, than to you he hath said,
To you, who for refuge to Jesus have fled?

2 " Fear not, I am with thee, oh, be not dismayed,
For I am thy God, I will still give thee aid :
I'll strengthen thee, help thee, and cause thee to stand,
Upheld by my gracious, omnipotent hand.

3 " When through fiery trials thy pathway shall lie,
My grace, all-sufficient, shall be thy supply,
The flame shall not hurt thee; I only design
Thy dross to consume, and thy gold to refine.

4 " The soul that on Jesus hath leaned for repose,
I will not—I will not desert to his foes;
That soul—though all hell should endeavor to shake,
I'll never—no never—no never forsake!"
KIRKHAM.

139.   " *Faint, yet pursuing.*"   11s.

THOUGH faint, yet pursuing, we go on our way;
The Lord is our Leader, his word is our stay;
Though suffering, and sorrow, and trial be near,
The Lord is our refuge, and whom can we fear?

2 He raiseth the fallen, he cheereth the faint;
The weak and oppressed—he will hear their complaint;
The way may be weary, and thorny the road,
But how can we falter? our help is in God!

3 And to his green pastures our footsteps he leads;
His flock in the desert how kindly he feeds!
The lambs in his bosom he tenderly bears,
And brings back the wanderers all safe from the snares.

4 Though clouds may surround us, our God is our light;
Though storms rage around us, our God is our might;
So faint, yet pursuing, still onward we come;
The Lord is our Leader, and heaven is our home!

140.   *"I will fear no evil."*   L. M. 6l.

THE Lord my pasture shall prepare,
And feed me with a shepherd's care;
His presence shall my wants supply,
And guard me with a watchful eye:
My noonday walks he shall attend,
And all my midnight hours defend.

2 When in the sultry glebe I faint,
Or on the thirsty mountain pant,
To fertile vales, and dewy meads,
My weary, wandering steps he leads;
Where peaceful rivers, soft and slow,
Amid the verdant landscape flow.

3 Though in the paths of death I tread,
With gloomy horrors overspread,

My steadfast heart shall fear no ill,
For thou, O Lord, art with me still;
Thy friendly rod shall give me aid,
And guide me through the dreadful shade.

4 Though in a bare and rugged way,
Through devious lonely wilds I stray,
Thy presence shall my pains beguile:
The barren wilderness shall smile,
With sudden greens and herbage crowned;
And streams shall murmur all around.
       ADDISON.

141. *The Good Shepherd.*   11s.

THE Lord is my Shepherd, how happy am I!
 How tender and watchful my wants to supply!
He daily provides me with raiment and food,
Whate'er he denies me is meant for my good.

2 The Lord is my Shepherd, how happy am I!
I'm blest while I live, and I'm blest when I die:
In death's gloomy valley no evil I'll dread,
For "I will be with thee," my Shepherd hath said.

3 The Lord is my Shepherd, I'll sing with delight,
Till called to adore him in regions of light:
Then praise him, with angels, to bright harps of gold,
And ever and ever his glory behold.

142.   Psalm xxiii.   11s.

THE Lord is my Shepherd, no want shall I know;
 I feed in green pastures; safe folded I rest:

He leadeth my soul where the still waters flow;
  Restores me when wandering, redeems when
    oppressed.

2 Through the valley of the shadow of death
    though I stray,
Since thou art my Guardian, no evil I fear;
Thy rod shall defend me, thy staff be my stay;
  No harm can befall with my Comforter near.
MONTGOMERY.

143.   *The Shepherd.*   S. M.

WHILE my Redeemer's near,
  My shepherd and my guide,
I bid farewell to anxious fear;
  My wants are all supplied.

2 To ever fragrant meads,
  Where rich abundance grows,
His gracious hand indulgent leads,
  And guards my sweet repose.

3 Dear Shepherd, if I stray,
  My wandering feet restore;
To thy fair pastures guide my way,
  And let me rove no more.
MRS. STEELE.

144.   Psalm xxiii.   C. M.

THE Lord himself, the mighty Lord,
  Vouchsafes to be my guide;
The Shepherd, by whose constant care
  My wants are all supplied.

2 In tender grass he makes me feed,
  And gently there repose;
Then leads me to cool shades, and where
  Refreshing water flows.

3 He does my wandering soul reclaim,
  And, to his endless praise,
Instruct with humble zeal to walk
  In his most righteous ways.

4 I pass the gloomy vale of death,
  From fear and danger free;
For there his aiding rod and staff
  Defend and comfort me.

VARIOUS PETITIONS.

145.   Gen. xxviii. 10-22.   6s. & 4s.

NEARER, my God, to thee,
  Nearer to thee:
Ev'n though it be a cross
  That raiseth me,
Still all my song shall be,
‖: Nearer, my God, to thee, :‖
  Nearer to thee.

2 Though like a wanderer,
  Daylight all gone,
Darkness be over me,
  My rest a stone,
Yet in my dreams I'd be
‖: Nearer, my God, to thee, :‖
  Nearer to thee.

3 There let the way appear
  Steps up to heaven;
All that thou sendest me
  In mercy given,
Angels to beckon me
‖: Nearer, my God, to thee, :‖
  Nearer to thee.   S. F. ADAMS.

146.   *"My Father, God."*   C. M.

LORD, I address thy heavenly throne;
  Call me a child of thine;
Send down the Spirit of thy Son,
  To form my heart divine.

2 There shed thy choicest love abroad,
  And make my comforts strong;
Then shall I say—"My Father, God,"
  With an unwav'ring tongue.   WATTS.

147.   *Divine Guidance sought.*   C. M.

OH, that the Lord would guide my ways
  To keep his statutes still!
Oh, that my God would grant me grace
  To know and do his will!

2 Order my footsteps by thy word,
  And make my heart sincere;
Let sin have no dominion, Lord,
  But keep my conscience clear.

3 Make me to walk in thy commands—
  'Tis a delightful road;
Nor let my head, nor heart, nor hands,
  Offend against my God.   WATTS.

148.   Psalm cxxxix. 23.   L. M.

GREAT God! my Father and my Friend,
  On whom I cast my constant care,
On whom for all things I depend!
  To thee I raise my humble prayer.

2 Endue me with a holy fear;
  The frailty of my heart reveal;
Sin and its snares are always near;
  Thee may I always nearer feel.

3 Search, gracious God! my inmost heart;
   From guilt and error set me free;
Thy light, and truth, and peace, impart,
   And guide me safe to heaven and thee.

149.   *Love Divine.*   8s. & 7s. D.

LOVE divine, all love excelling—
   Joy of heaven! to earth come down!
Fix in us thy humble dwelling,
   All thy faithful mercies crown:
Jesus! thou art all compassion,
   Pure, unbounded love thou art;
Visit us with thy salvation,
   Enter every trembling heart.

2 Breathe, oh, breathe thy loving Spirit
   Into every troubled breast!
Let us all in thee inherit,
   Let us find thy promised rest:
Come, almighty to deliver,
   Let us all thy life receive!
Speedily return, and never,
   Never more thy temples leave!

3 Finish then thy new creation,
   Pure, unspotted may we be:
Let us see our whole salvation
   Perfectly secured by thee!
Changed from glory into glory,
   Till in heaven we take our place;
Till we cast our crowns before thee,
   Lost in wonder, love, and praise.
                              C. WESLEY.

150.   Psalm xxii.   C. M.

OH, help us, Lord; each hour of need
   Thy heavenly succor give;

Help us in thought, and word, and deed,
  Each hour on earth we live.

2 Oh, help us when our spirits bleed
    With contrite anguish sore;
  And when our hearts are cold and dead,
    Oh, help us, Lord, the more.

3 Oh, help us through the prayer of faith
    More firmly to believe;
  For still the more the servant hath
    The more he shall receive.

4 Oh, help us, Jesus, from on high;
    We know no help but thee;
  Oh, help us so to live and die
    As thine in heaven to be.   MILMAN.

151.   Deut. xxxiii. 27.   8s. & 7s. D.

HOLY Father, thou hast taught me
  I should live to thee alone;
Year by year thy hand hath brought me
  On through dangers oft unknown.
When I wandered, thou hast found me;
  When I doubted, sent me light;
Still thine arm has been around me,
  All my paths were in thy sight.

2 I would trust in thy protection,
    Wholly rest upon thine arm;
  Follow wholly thy direction,
    Thou, mine only guard from harm!
  Keep me from mine own undoing,
    Help me turn to thee when tried,
  Still my footsteps, Father, viewing,
    Keep me ever at thy side!

152.   Psalm xxxi.   L. M.

LORD, in thy great, thy glorious name,
  I place my hope, my only trust;
Save me from sorrow, guilt and shame,
  Thou ever gracious, ever just.

2 Thou art my Rock! thy name alone
  The fortress where my hopes retreat;
Oh, make thy power and mercy known;
  To safety guide my wandering feet.

3 Blest be the Lord, forever blest,
  Whose mercy bids my fears remove;
The sacred walls which guard my rest
  Are his almighty power and love.
Mrs. Steele.

153.   *Prayer for Strength.*   11s. & 10s.

LORD, we have wandered forth through doubt
    and sorrow,
And thou hast made each step an onward one,
And we will ever trust each unknown morrow—
  Thou wilt sustain us till its work is done.

2 O Father, now in thy dear presence kneeling,
  Our spirits yearn to feel thy kindling love;
Now make us strong thro' thine own deep revealing
  Of trust and strength and calmness from above.

154.   *Prayer for Guidance.*   8s. 7s. & 4s.

GUIDE me, O thou great Jehovah,
  Pilgrim through this barren land;
I am weak, but thou art mighty;
  Hold me with thy powerful hand;
    Bread of heaven,
Feed me till I want no more.

2 Open thou the crystal fountain
   Whence the healing streams do flow;
Let the fiery, cloudy pillar
   Lead me all my journey through;
      Strong Deliverer,
Be thou still my Strength and Shield.

3 When I tread the verge of Jordan,
   Bid my anxious fears subside;
Death of death! and hell's destruction!
   Land me safe on Canaan's side;
      Songs of praises
I will ever give to thee.   OLIVER.

155.   John xvii. 9.   7s.

THINE forever! God of Love,
   Hear us from thy throne above!
Thine forever may we be,
Here and in eternity!

2 Thine forever! oh, how blest
They who find in thee their rest!
Saviour, Guardian, heavenly Friend,
Oh, defend us to the end!

3 Thine forever! Saviour, keep
These thy frail and trembling sheep;
Safe alone beneath thy care,
Let us all thy goodness share.

4 Thine forever! thou our Guide;
All our wants by thee supplied—
All our sins by thee forgiven—
Lead us, Lord, from earth to heaven!

156.   Psalm xci. 11.   8s. 7s. & 4s.

KEEP us, Lord, oh, keep us ever!
   Vain our hope, if left by thee;

We are thine; oh, leave us never,
   Till thy glorious face we see!
      Then to praise thee
   Through a bright eternity.

2 Precious is thy word of promise,
   Precious to thy people here;
Never take thy presence from us,
   Jesus, Saviour, still be near:
      Living, dying,
   May thy name our spirits cheer.

157. *Seeking Strength for Duty.* C. M.

JEHOVAH! by thy covenant
   With all thy people made,
We come to ask thee that our hearts
   Upon thy truth be stayed.

2 Ere entering on the battle-field,
   In struggle stern, of life,
We ask thee, for thy glory's sake,
   Be with us in the strife.

3 Oh, strengthen thou our purposes
   To struggle and to be;
May all our thoughts, and words, and works,
   Be sacred still to thee.

4 Give us the force to will, to work,
   No suffering to shun,
And by our efforts, Lord of Hosts,
   Oh, let thy will be done.
                    LUCY E. GUERNSEY.

158. *Divine Help.* C. M.

O GRACIOUS God! in whom I live,
   My feeble efforts aid;

Help me to watch, and pray, and strive,
  Though trembling and afraid.

2 Increase my faith, increase my hope,
  When foes and fears prevail;
And bear my fainting spirit up,
  Or soon my strength will fail.

3 Oh, keep me in thy heavenly way,
  And bid the tempter flee!
And let me never, never stray
  From happiness and thee.
                              MRS. STEELE.

159.   *Heavenly Wisdom Implored.*   C. M.

FATHER of light, conduct my feet
  Through life's dark, dangerous road;
Let each advancing step still bring
  Me nearer to my God.

2 Teach me in every various scene
  To keep my end in sight;
And, while I tread life's mazy track,
  Let wisdom guide me right.

3 That heavenly wisdom from above
  Abundantly impart;
And let it guard, and guide, and warm,
  And penetrate my heart;

4 Till it shall lead me to thyself,
  Fountain of bliss and love!
And all my darkness be dispersed
  In endless light above.   SMART.

160.   *The Lord's Prayer.*   C. M.

OUR Father, God, who art in heaven,
  All hallowed be thy name!

Thy kingdom come: thy will be done,
  In earth and heaven the same!

2 Give us this day our daily bread;
  And, as we those forgive
Who sin against us, so may we
  Forgiving grace receive.

3 Into temptation lead us not;
  From evil set us free;
And thine the kingdom, thine the power
  And glory ever be.   JUDSON.

161.   Psalm xviii. 35.   8s. & 7s.

GENTLY, Lord, oh, gently lead us
  Through this lonely vale of tears;
Thro' the changes thou'st decreed us,
  Till our last great change appears.

2 When temptation's darts assail us,
  When in devious paths we stray,
Let thy goodness never fail us,
  Lead us in thy perfect way.

3 In the hour of pain and anguish,
  In the hour when death draws near,
Suffer not our hearts to languish—
  Suffer not our souls to fear.

4 And, when mortal life is ended,
  Bid us on thy bosom rest,
Till, by angel-bands attended,
  We awake among the blest.
                     HASTINGS.

162.   *Courage.*   8s. & 7s.

FATHER, hear the prayer we offer!
  Not for ease that prayer shall be,

But for strength that we may ever
　Live our lives courageously.

2 Not forever by still waters
　Would we idly quiet stay;
But would smite the living fountains
　From the rocks along our way.

3 Be our strength in hours of weakness,
　In our wanderings be our guide;
Through endeavor, failure, danger,
　Father, be thou at our side!

163.　　*Giving the Heart.*　　8s. & 7s.

TAKE my heart, O Father, take it!
　Make and keep it all thine own;
Let thy Spirit melt and break it—
　This proud heart of sin and stone.

2 Father, make it pure and lowly,
　Fond of peace, and far from strife;
Turning from the paths unholy
　Of this vain and sinful life.

3 Ever let thy grace surround it;
　Strengthen it with power divine,
Till thy cords of love have bound it:
　Make it to be wholly thine.

164.　　*Resignation.*　　C. M.

MY God, my Father, blissful name!
　Oh, may I call thee mine?
May I with sweet assurance claim
　A portion so divine?

2 Whate'er thy providence denies
　I calmly would resign;

For thou art good, and just, and wise:
  Oh, bend my will to thine!

3 Whate'er thy sacred will ordains,
  Oh, give me strength to bear!
And let me know my Father reigns,
  And trust his tender care.
                         MRS. STEELE.

165.   *Repentance.*   7s.

GOD of mercy! God of love!
  Hear our sad, repentant song;
Sorrow dwells on every face,
  Penitence on every tongue.

2 Deep regret for follies past,
  Talents wasted, time misspent;
Hearts debased by worldly cares,
  Thankless for the blessings lent;

3 These, and every secret fault,
  Filled with grief and shame, we own;
Humbled at thy feet we lie,
  Seeking pardon from thy throne.

4 God of mercy! God of grace!
  Hear our sad, repentant songs;
Oh, restore thy suppliant race,
  Thou to whom all praise belongs!
                         J. TAYLOR.

166.   *Repentance.*   5s. & 4s.

JESUS, most holy,
  Pray I to thee;
My sinful fetters,
  Lord, break from me;
Take this sad spirit,
  Mourning for sin,

Back to thy bosom,
  Lord, take me in.

2 Over the mountains
  Long have I strayed;
Cold winds of sorrow
  Round me have played;
None to bring comfort,
  None have I found;
While tears of anguish
  Watered the ground.

3 To this dear refuge
  Now have I fled;
Jesus, thy kind heart
  For me hath bled;
Take now the wanderer
  Home to thy rest,
Under thy kind wings
  Sheltered and blest.

167.   1 John v. 14, 15.   C. M.

LORD! when we bend before thy throne,
  And our confessions pour,
Oh, may we feel the sins we own,
  And hate what we deplore.

2 Our contrite spirits pitying see;
  True penitence impart:
And let a healing ray from thee
  Beam hope on every heart.

3 When we disclose our wants in prayer,
  May we our wills resign;
Nor let a thought our bosom share,
  Which is not wholly thine.

4 Let faith each meek petition fill,
  And waft it to the skies;

And teach our heart 'tis goodness still
  That grants it or denies.

168. *Solomon's Prayer for Wisdom.*   C. M.

ALMIGHTY God, in humble prayer
  To thee our souls we lift;
Do thou our waiting minds prepare
  For thy most needful gift.

2 We ask not golden streams of wealth
  Along our path to flow;
We ask not undecaying health,
  Nor length of years below.

3 We ask not honors, which an hour
  May bring and take away;
We ask not pleasure, pomp, and power
  Lest we should go astray.

4 We ask for wisdom: Lord, impart
  The knowledge how to live;
A wise and understanding heart
  To all before thee give.
                MONTGOMERY.

169.   Psalm li. 10.   C. M.

OH, for a heart to praise my God,
  A heart from sin set free;
A heart that's sprinkled with the blood
  So freely shed for me!

2 A heart in every thought renewed,
  And filled with love divine;
Perfect, and right, and pure, and good;
  An image, Lord! of thine.

3 Thy nature, gracious Lord! impart;
  Come quickly from above;

Write thy new name upon my heart—
Thy new, best name of Love.
                                C. WESLEY.

170.   *Seeking Peace.*   L. M. 6l.

O FATHER! lift our souls above,
   Till we find rest in thy dear love;
And still that peace divine impart
Which sanctifies the inmost heart,
And makes each morn and setting sun
But bring us nearer to thy throne.

2 May we our daily duties meet,
Tread sin each day beneath our feet,
And win that strength which doth thy will,
And seeth thee, and so is still;
And, fixed on thy sustaining arm,
Find daily food and know no harm.

3 Help us with man in peace to live,
Our brother's wrong in love forgive,
And day and night the tempter flee
Through strength which comes alone from
     thee!
Thus will our spirits find their rest
In thy deep peace forever blest.

171.   *" Perfect us in Love."*   C. M.

TRY us, O God, and search the ground
    Of every sinful heart;
Whate'er of sin in us is found,
   Oh, bid it all depart.

2 Help us to help each other, Lord,
   Each other's cross to bear;

Let each his friendly aid afford,
  And feel his brother's care.

3 Help us to build each other up,
  Our heart and life improve;
Increase our faith, confirm our hope,
  And perfect us in love.

4 Up into thee, our living Head,
  Let us in all things grow,
Till thou hast made us free, indeed,
  And spotless here below. C. WESLEY.

172.   *Happiness in God only.*   C. M

IN vain I trace creation o'er,
  In search of solid rest:
The whole creation is too poor,
  Too mean, to make me blest.

2 Let earth and all her charms depart,
  Unworthy of the mind:
In God alone this restless heart
  Enduring bliss can find.

3 Thy favor, Lord, is all I want;
  Here would my spirit rest:
Oh, seal the rich, the boundless grant,
  And make me fully blest!
        MRS. STEELE.

173.   *"Not my will, but Thine."*   C. M.

AUTHOR of good! to thee we turn:
  Thine ever-wakeful eye
Alone can all our wants discern—
  Thy hand alone supply.

2 Oh, let thy love within us dwell,
  Thy fear our footsteps guide;

That love shall vainer loves expel,
  That fear all fears beside.

3 And since, by passion's force subdued,
   Too oft with stubborn will
We blindly shun the latent good,
   And grasp the specious ill;

4 Not what we wish, but what we want,
   Let mercy still supply;
The good we ask not, Father, grant;
   The ill we ask, deny.   MERRICK.

174.   *Subjection to the Divine Will.*   L. M.

O THOU, who hast at thy command
  The hearts of all men in thy hand!
Our wayward, erring hearts incline
To have no other will but thine.

2 Our wishes, our desires, control;
Mould every purpose of the soul;
O'er all may we victorious be
That stands between ourselves and thee.

3 Thrice blest will all our blessings be,
When we can look through them to thee;
When each glad heart its tribute pays
Of love, and gratitude, and praise.
                          MRS. COTTERILL.

175.   Luke xxiii. 42.   C. M.

O THOU, from whom all goodness flows,
  I lift my soul to thee;
In all my sorrows, conflicts, woes,
  O Lord, remember me!

2 When on my aching, burdened heart
   My sins lie heavily,

Thy pardon grant, new peace impart;
 Thus, Lord, remember me!

3 When trials sore obstruct my way,
 And ills I can not flee,
Oh, let my strength be as my day—
 Dear Lord, remember me!

4 When in the solemn hour of death
 I wait thy just decree;
Be this the prayer of my last breath:
 Now, Lord, remember me!

176. Prov. xxiii. 26. C. M.

MY God, accept my heart this day,
 And make it always thine;
That I from thee no more may stray,
 No more from thee decline.

2 Let every thought, and work, and word
 To thee be ever given;
Then life shall be thy service, Lord,
 And death the gate of heaven!
 LYRA CATH.

177. *" The Lord is my Light."* L. M. 6l.

GRANT us, dear Lord, from evil ways
 True absolution and release;
And bless us more than in past days,
 With purity and inward peace.
Thro' life's long day and death's dark night,
O gentle Jesus, be our Light.
Chorus: Through the day, through the night,
O gentle Jesus, be our Light.

2 Do more than pardon; give us joy,
 Sweet fear, and sober liberty,

  And simple hearts without alloy
   That only long to be like thee.
 Thro' life's long day and death's dark night,
 O gentle Jesus, be our Light.
   Chorus: Through, etc.

3 Labor is sweet, for thou hast toiled;
  And care is light, for thou hast cared;
Ah! never let our works be soiled
  With strife, or by deceit ensnared.
Thro' life's long day and death's dark night,
O gentle Jesus, be our Light.
  Chorus: Through, etc.

4 For all we love—the poor, the sad,
  The sinful—unto thee we call;
Oh, let thy mercy make us glad:
  Thou art our Jesus, and our All.
Thro' life's long day and death's dark night,
O gentle Jesus, be our Light.
  Chorus: Through, etc.
MONK'S COLL.

178.   *The Safe Retreat.*   C. M.

DEAR Father, to thy mercy-seat
 My soul for shelter flies:
'Tis here I find a safe retreat
 When storms and tempests rise.

 2 My cheerful hope can never die,
  If thou, my God, art near;
 Thy grace can raise my comforts high,
  And banish every fear.

 3 My great Protector and my Lord,
  Thy constant aid impart;

Oh, let thy kind, thy gracious word
  Sustain my trembling heart!

4 Oh, never let my soul remove
  From this divine retreat!
Still let me trust thy power and love,
  And dwell beneath thy feet.
                                MRS. STEELE.

179.   *Prayer for Contentment.*   C. M.

FATHER! whate'er of earthly bliss
  Thy sovereign hand denies,
Accepted at thy throne of grace,
  Let this petition rise:

2 "Give me a calm, a thankful heart,
  From every murmur free;
The blessings of thy grace impart,
  And make me live to thee.

3 "Let the sweet hope that thou art mine
  My life and death attend;
Thy presence through my journey shine,
  And crown my journey's end."
                                MRS. STEELE.

180.   *The Good Shepherd.*   7s.

JESUS, Shepherd of the sheep;
  Powerful is thine arm to keep
All thy flocks with safest care,
Fed in pastures large and fair.

2 Thee their Guide and Guard they own;
Thee they love, and thee alone;
Thee they follow day by day,
Fearful lest their feet should stray.

3 Lord, thy helpless sheep behold;
Gather all unto thy fold;
Gently lead the wanderers home;
Watch them, lest again they roam.

4 Bring thy sheep, now far astray,
Lost in Satan's evil way;
Then, the fold and shepherd one,
We shall praise thee round the throne.

181. *Imitation of Christ in Youth.* 6s.

I FEEL within a want
  Forever burning there;
What I so thirst for, grant,
  O Thou who hearest prayer!

2 This is the thing I crave:
  A likeness to thy Son;
This would I rather have
  Than call the world my own.

3 Like him, now in my youth,
  I long, O God, to be—
In tenderness and truth,
  In sweet humility.

4 'Tis my most fervent prayer:
  Be it more fervent still—
Be it my highest care:
  Be it my settled will!   FURNESS.

182. *Example of the "Wise Men."* 7s. 6l.

AS with gladness men of old
  Did the guiding star behold;
As with joy they hailed its light,
Leading onward, beaming bright;

So, most gracious Lord, may we
Evermore be led by thee.

2 As with joyful steps they sped
To that lowly manger-bed;
There to bend the knee before
Him whom heaven and earth adore;
So may we with willing feet
Ever seek the mercy-seat.

3 As they offered gifts most rare
At that manger rude and bare;
So may we with holy joy,
Pure and free from sin's alloy,
All our costliest treasures bring,
Christ! to thee, our heavenly King.

4 Holy Jesus, every day
Keep us in the narrow way;
And, when earthly things are past,
Bring our ransomed souls at last
Where they need no star to guide,
Where no clouds thy glory hide.

183. 1 Peter i. 8. 6s. & 4s.

SAVIOUR! thy gentle voice
  Gladly we hear;
Author of all our joys,
  Ever be near;
Our souls would cling to thee,
Let us thy fullness see,
  Our life to cheer.

2 Fountain of life divine!
  Thee we adore;
We would be wholly thine
  Forevermore;

Freely forgive our sin,
　　Grant heavenly peace within,
　　　Thy light restore.
　3 Though to our faith unseen,
　　While darkness reigns,
　On thee alone we lean
　　While life remains;
　By thy free grace restored,
　Our souls shall bless the Lord
　　In joyful strains!　　　Hastings.

184.　　　Luke v. 11.　　　5s. & 8s.

　　JESUS, still lead on,
　　　Till our rest be won:
　And although the way be cheerless,
　We will follow calm and fearless;
　　Guide us by thy hand
　　To our Fatherland!

　2 If the way be drear,
　　If the foe be near,
　Let not faithless fears o'ertake us;
　Let not faith and hope forsake us;
　　For, through many a foe,
　　To our home we go!

　3 When we seek relief
　　From a long-felt grief:
　When temptations come alluring,
　Make us patient and enduring:
　　Show us that bright shore
　　Where we weep no more!

　4 Jesus, still lead on,
　　Till our rest be won;
　Heavenly Leader, still direct us,
　Still support, console, protect us,

Till we safely stand
In our Fatherland! ZINZENDORF.

185. *Trust in Jesus.* C. M.

JESUS, in sickness and in pain
Be near to succor me;
My sinking spirit still sustain:
To thee I turn, to thee.

2 When cares and sorrows thicken round,
And nothing bright I see,
In thee alone can help be found;
To thee I turn, to thee.

3 Should strong temptations fierce assail,
And Satan buffet me,
Then in thy strength will I prevail,
While still I turn to thee.

4 Through all my pilgrimage below,
Whate'er my lot may be,
In joy or sadness, weal or woe,
Jesus, I'll turn to thee. GALLAUDET.

186. *Confidence in God's Care.* 7s.

TO thy pastures, fair and large,
Heavenly Shepherd, lead thy charge;
And my couch, with tenderest care,
'Mid the springing grass prepare.

2 When I faint with summer's heat,
Thou shalt guide my weary feet
To the streams that, still and slow,
Through the verdant meadows flow.

3 Safe the dreary vale I tread,
By the shades of death o'erspread,

With thy rod and staff supplied—
This my guard, and that my guide.

4 Constant to my latest end
Thou my footsteps shalt attend;
Thou shalt bid thy hallowed dome
Yield me an eternal home.   MERRICK.

187.   Isaiah xl. 11.   8s. 7s. & 4s.

SAVIOUR, like a shepherd lead us,
  Much we need thy tender care:
In thy pleasant pastures feed us;
  For our use thy folds prepare:
    Blessed Jesus!
  Thou hast bought us, thine we are.

2 Thou hast promised to receive us;
  Poor and sinful though we be;
Thou hast mercy to relieve us,
  Grace to cleanse, and power to free:
    Blessed Jesus!
  Let us early turn to thee.

3 Early let us seek thy favor;
  Early let us learn thy will;
Do thou, Lord, our only Saviour,
  With thy love our bosoms fill:
    Blessed Jesus!
  Thou hast loved us,—love us still!

188.   *Consecration.*—Rom. xii. 1.   L. M.

JESUS! our best beloved Friend,
  On thy redeeming name we call;
Jesus! in love to us descend,
  Pardon and sanctify us all.

2 Our souls and bodies we resign,
   To fear and follow thy commands;
 Oh! take our hearts, our hearts are thine,
   Accept the service of our hands.

3 Firm, faithful, watching unto prayer,
   Our Master's voice will we obey,
 Toil in the vineyard here, and bear
   The heat and burden of the day.

4 Yet, Lord, for us a resting-place,
   In heaven, at thy right hand, prepare;
 And, till we see thee face to face,
   Be all our conversation there.

189.   *Christ a Refuge.*   7s. D.

JESUS, Lover of my soul,
   Let me to thy bosom fly,
While the waters near me roll,
   While the tempest still is high:
Hide me, O my Saviour, hide,
   Till the storm of life is past;
Safe into the haven guide:
   Oh, receive my soul at last!

2 Other refuge have I none;
   Hangs my helpless soul on thee:
 Leave, ah! leave me not alone;
   Still support and comfort me:
 All my trust on thee is stayed,
   All my help from thee I bring;
 Cover my defenseless head
   With the shadow of thy wing.
                              C. WESLEY.

190.   *For God's Presence.*   7s.

LORD, it is not life to live,
   If thy presence thou deny;

Lord, if thou thy presence give,
'Tis no longer death to die.

2 Source and Giver of repose,
Singly from thy smile it flows;
Peace and happiness are thine,
Mine they are, if thou art mine.
TOPLADY.

191. *For God's Presence.* C. M.

FATHER in heaven, to whom our hearts
Would lift themselves in prayer,
Drive from our souls each earthly thought,
And show thy presence there.

2 Each moment of our lives renews
The mercies of the Lord;
Each moment is itself a gift
To bear us on to God.

3 Help us to break the galling chains
This world has round us thrown;
Each passion of our hearts subdue,
Each cherished sin disown.

4 O Father! kindle in our souls
A never-dying flame,
Of holy love, of grateful trust
In thine almighty name. H. WARE, JR.

192. *Prayer for Guidance.* 8s. 7s. & 4s.

LEAD us, heavenly Father, lead us
O'er the world's tempestuous sea;
Guard us, guide us, keep us, feed us,
For we have no help but thee;
Yet possessing
Every blessing,
If our God our Father be.

2 Saviour, breathe forgiveness o'er us;
  All our weakness thou dost know;
Thou didst tread the earth before us;
  Thou didst feel its keenest woe;
    Lone and dreary,
    Faint and weary,
Through the desert thou didst go.

3 Spirit of our God, descending,
  Fill our hearts with heavenly joy;
Love with every passion blending,
  Pleasure that can never cloy;
    Thus provided,
    Pardoned, guided,
Nothing can our peace destroy.

193.   *Watch unto Prayer.*   S. M.

O GOD! my Strength, my Hope,
  On thee I cast my care,
With humble confidence look up,
  And know thou hearest prayer.

2 Oh, for a godly fear,
  A quick, discerning eye
That looks to thee when sin is near,
  And sees the tempter fly!

3 Lord let me still abide,
  Nor from my hope remove,
Till thou my patient spirit guide
  Into thy perfect love.   C. WESLEY.

194.   2 Cor. i. 22.   7s

GRACIOUS Spirit, Love divine!
  Let thy light within me shine;
All my guilty fears remove,
Fill me with thy heavenly love.

2 Life and peace to me impart,
Seal salvation on my heart;
Breathe thyself into my breast,
Earnest of immortal rest.

3 Let me never from thee stray,
Keep me in the narrow way;
Fill my soul with joy divine,
Keep me, Lord, forever thine.
STOCKER.

195. *Prayer for Guidance.* L. M.

COME, gracious Spirit, heavenly Dove,
With light and comfort from above;
Be thou our guardian, thou our guide,
O'er every thought and step preside.

2 The light of truth to us display,
And make us know and choose thy way;
Plant holy fear in every heart,
That we from God may ne'er depart.

3 Lead us to holiness—the road
Which we must take to dwell with God;
Lead us to Christ, the living way,
Nor let us from his pastures stray.

4 Lead us to God, our final rest,
To be with him forever blest;
Lead us to heaven, its bliss to share—
Fullness of joy forever there! BROWNE.

196. *Boldness in Prayer.* S. M.

BEHOLD the throne of grace:
The promise calls me near;
There Jesus shows a smiling face,
And waits to answer prayer.

2 Thine image, Lord, bestow,
    Thy presence and thy love;
  I ask to serve thee here below,
    And reign with thee above.

3 Teach me to live by faith;
    Conform my will to thine;
  Let me victorious be in death,
    And then in glory shine. NEWTON.

197.   Luke xviii. 1.   S. M.

JESUS, who knows full well
    The heart of every saint,
  Invites us all our grief to tell,
    To pray and never faint.

2 He bows his gracious ear—
    We never plead in vain;
  Then let us wait till he appear,
    And pray, and pray again.

3 Jesus, the Lord, will hear
    His chosen when they cry;
  Yes, though he may awhile forbear,
    He'll help them from on high.

4 Then let us earnest cry,
    And never faint in prayer;
  He sees, he hears, and, from on high,
    Will make our cause his care.
                          NEWTON.

198.   Matt. vii. 7.   7s

COME, my soul, thy suit prepare,
  Jesus loves to answer prayer;
He himself invites thee near,
Bids thee ask him, waits to hear.

2 Lord! I come to thee for rest,
Take possession of my breast;
There thy sovereign right maintain,
And, without a rival, reign.

3 While I am a pilgrim here,
Let thy love my spirit cheer;
Be my Guide, my Guard, my Friend,
Lead me to my journey's end.

4 Show me what I have to do,
Every hour my strength renew;
Let me live a life of faith,
Let me die thy people's death.
NEWTON.

199.   Eph. vi. 18.   7s

THEY who seek the throne of grace
Find that throne in every place;
If we live a life of prayer,
God is present everywhere.

2 In our sickness and our health,
In our want, or in our wealth,
If we look to God in prayer,
God is present everywhere.

3 When our earthly comforts fail,
When the foes of life prevail,
'Tis the time for earnest prayer;
God is present everywhere.

4 Then, my soul, in every strait,
To thy Father come, and wait;
He will answer every prayer:
God is present everywhere.

DUTIES AND PRIVILEGES.

200. *Hour of Prayer.* L. M. D.

SWEET hour of prayer, sweet hour of prayer,
That calls me from a world of care,
And bids me at my Father's throne
Make all my wants and wishes known;
In seasons of distress and grief
My soul has often found relief,
And oft escaped the tempter's snare,
By thy return, sweet hour of prayer.

2 Sweet hour of prayer, sweet hour of prayer,
Thy wings shall my petition bear
To Him whose truth and faithfulness
Engage the waiting soul to bless:
And since he bids me seek his face,
Believe his word, and trust his grace,
I'll cast on him my every care,
And wait for thee, sweet hour of prayer.

RELIGIOUS DUTIES AND PRIVILEGES.

201. *"Watch and Pray."* S. M.

MY soul! be on thy guard;
Ten thousand foes arise;
The hosts of sin are pressing hard
To draw thee from the skies.

2 Oh, watch, and fight, and pray!
The battle ne'er give o'er;
Renew it boldly every day,
And help divine implore.

3 Ne'er think the victory won,
Nor once at ease sit down;

Thy arduous work will not be done
  Till thou obtain thy crown.

4 Fight on, my soul, till death
    Shall bring thee to thy God!
  He'll take thee, at thy parting breath,
    Up to his blest abode. HEATH.

202. *The Heavenly Race.* C. M.

AWAKE, my soul! stretch every nerve,
    And press with vigor on:
  A heavenly race demands thy zeal,
  A bright, immortal crown.

2 A cloud of witnesses around
    Hold thee in full survey;
  Forget the steps already trod,
    And onward urge thy way.

3 'Tis God's all-animating voice
    That calls thee from on high;
  'Tis his own hand presents the prize
    To thine aspiring eye.

4 Blest Saviour, introduced by thee,
    Have I my race begun;
  And, crowned with victory, at thy feet
    I'll lay my honors down.
          DODDRIDGE.

203. Isaiah xl. 28–31. L. M.

AWAKE, our souls! away, our fears!
    Let every trembling thought be gone;
  Awake, and run the heavenly race,
    And put a cheerful courage on!

2 True, 'tis a strait and thorny road,
    And mortal spirits tire and faint;

But they forget the mighty God,
   Who feeds the strength of every saint.

3 From thee, the overflowing spring,
   Our souls shall drink a fresh supply;
While such as trust their native strength
   Shall melt away, and droop, and die.

4 Swift as an eagle cuts the air
   We'll mount aloft to thine abode;
On wings of love our souls shall fly,
   Nor tire amid the heavenly road!
                              WATTS.

204.   *Patience and Hope.*   8s. & 7s. D.

KNOW, my soul, thy full salvation;
   Rise o'er sin, and fear, and care;
Joy to find in every station
   Something still to do or bear:
Think what Spirit dwells within thee;
   Think what Father's smiles are thine;
Think that Jesus died to win thee;
   Child of heaven, canst thou repine?

2 Haste thee on from grace to glory,
   Armed by faith, and winged by prayer;
Heaven's eternal day before thee—
   God's own hand shall guide thee there.
Soon shall close thine earthly mission,
   Soon shall pass thy pilgrim days;
Hope shall change to glad fruition,
   Faith to sight and prayer to praise.
                           MISS GRANT.

205.   *A Good Conscience.*   L. M.

SWEET peace of conscience, heavenly
      guest,
Come, fix thy mansion in my breast;

Dispel my doubts, my fears control,
And heal the anguish of my soul.

2 Come, smiling hope, and joy sincere,
Come, make your constant dwelling here;
Still let your presence cheer my heart,
Nor sin compel you to depart.

3 O God of hope and peace divine,
Make thou these secret pleasures mine;
Forgive my sins, my fears remove,
And fill my heart with joy and love.
HEGINBOTHAM.

206. *Self-denial.* 8s. & 7s.

PILGRIMS in this vale of sorrow,
  Pressing onward toward the prize,
Strength and comfort here we borrow
  From the Hand that rules the skies.

2 'Mid these scenes of self-denial
  We are called the race to run;
We must meet full many a trial
  Ere the victor's crown is won.

3 Love shall every conflict lighten,
  Hope shall urge us swifter on,
Faith shall every prospect brighten,
  Till the morn of heaven shall dawn.

4 On the Eternal arm reclining,
  We at length shall win the day;
All the powers of earth combining,
  Shall not snatch our crown away.
HASTINGS.

207. *Blessing to the Contrite.* C. M.

COME, let us to the Lord our God
  With contrite hearts return!

Our God is gracious, nor will leave
   The desolate to mourn.

2 Our hearts, if God we seek to know,
   Shall know him and rejoice:
His coming like the morn shall be;
   Like morning songs his voice.

3 As dew upon the tender herb,
   Diffusing fragrance round;
As showers that usher in the spring,
   And cheer the thirsty ground:

4 So shall his presence bless our souls,
   And shed a joyful light;
That hallowed morn shall chase away
   The sorrows of the night.   MORRISON.

208.   *Humility.*   C. M.

THY home is with the humble, Lord!
   The simplest are the best;
Thy lodging is in child-like hearts;
   Thou makest there thy rest.

2 Dear Comforter! eternal Love!
   If thou wilt stay with me,
Of lowly thoughts and simple ways
   I'll build a house for thee.

3 Who made this beating heart of mine
   But thou, my heavenly Guest?
Let no one have it, then, but thee,
   And let it be thy rest!

209.   Matt. v. 8.   S. M.

BLEST are the pure in heart,
   For they shall see their God:

The secret of the Lord is theirs;
     Their soul is Christ's abode.

   2 He to the lowly soul
       Doth still himself impart,
     And for his dwelling, and his throne,
       Chooseth the pure in heart.

   3 Lord, we thy presence seek:
       May ours this blessing be;
     Oh, give the pure and lowly heart,
       A temple meet for thee!

210. *Wisdom.* C. M.

   OH, happy is the man that hears
       Instruction's warning voice;
     And who celestial wisdom makes
       His early, only choice.

   2 For she hath treasures greater far
       Than east and west unfold;
     And her rewards more precious are
       Than all their stores of gold.

   3 She guides the young with innocence
       In pleasure's paths to tread;
     A crown of glory she bestows
       Upon the hoary head.

   4 According as her labors rise,
       So her rewards increase;
     Her ways are ways of pleasantness,
       And all her paths are peace.   LOGAN.

211. *Resignation.* C. M. D.

   WHILE thee I seek, protecting Power!
       Be my vain wishes stilled;

And may this consecrated hour
  With better hopes be filled!
Thy love the power of thought bestowed;
  To thee my thoughts would soar:
Thy mercy o'er my life has flowed;
  That mercy I adore.

2 In each event of life, how clear
  Thy ruling hand I see!
Each blessing to my soul more dear,
  Because conferred by thee.
In every joy that crowns my days,
  In every pain I bear,
My heart shall find delight in praise,
  Or seek relief in prayer.

3 When gladness wings my favored hour,
  Thy love my thoughts shall fill;
Resigned, when storms of sorrow lower,
  My soul shall meet thy will.
My lifted eye, without a tear,
  The gathering storm shall see;
My steadfast heart shall know no fear;
  That heart will rest on thee.
              MISS WILLIAMS.

212. *Rejoicing in Hope.*   S. M.

COME, we who love the Lord,
  And let our joys be known;
Join in a song of sweet accord,
  And thus surround the throne.

2 The hill of Zion yields
  A thousand sacred sweets
Before we reach the heavenly fields,
  Or walk the golden streets.

3 Then let our songs abound,
   And every tear be dry;
We're marching through Immanuel's
     ground
   To fairer worlds on high.   WATTS.

213. *The Voice of Jesus.*   7s.

COME, said Jesus' sacred voice,
   Come, and make my paths your choice;
I will guide you to your home;
Weary wanderer, hither come.

2 Hither come! for here is found
Balm that flows for every wound;
Peace that ever shall endure,
Rest eternal, sacred, sure.   BARBAULD.

214. *Living by Faith Only.*   S. M.

IF through unruffled seas
   Toward heaven we calmly sail,
With grateful hearts, O God, to thee,
   We'll own the fostering gale.

2 But should the surges rise,
   And rest delay to come,
Blest be the sorrow, kind the storm,
   Which drives us nearer home.

3 Soon shall our doubts and fears
   All yield to thy control;
Thy tender mercies shall illume
   The midnight of the soul.

4 Teach us, in every state
   To make thy will our own;
And, when the joys of sense depart,
   To live by faith alone.

215. *Upward!* 6s.

Go up, go up, my heart!
  Dwell with thy God above;
For here thou canst not rest,
  Nor here give out thy love.

2 Go up, go up, my heart!
  Be not a trifler here;
Ascend above these clouds—
  Dwell in a higher sphere.

3 Let not thy love flow out
  To things so soiled and dim,
Go up to heaven and God;
  Take up thy love to him.

4 Waste not thy precious stores
  On pleasure here below:
To God that wealth belongs;
  On him that wealth bestow.
                              BONAR.

216. *Trust in Christ.* S. M.

My spirit on thy care,
  Blest Saviour, I recline;
Thou wilt not leave me to despair,
  For thou art love divine.

2 In thee I place my trust;
  On thee I calmly rest:
I know thee good, I know thee just,
  And count thy choice the best.

3 Whate'er events betide,
  Thy will they all perform;
Safe in thy breast my head I hide,
  Nor fear the coming storm.

4 Let good or ill befall,
    It must be good for me—
Secure of having thee in all,
    Of having all in thee.   LYTE.

217.   *Resignation.*   6s. D.

MY Jesus, as thou wilt!
    Oh, may thy will be mine!
Into thy hand of love
    I would my all resign:
Through sorrow, or through joy,
    Conduct me as thine own,
And help me still to say,
    My Lord, thy will be done!

2 My Jesus, as thou wilt!
    All shall be well for me:
Each changing future scene
    I gladly trust with thee:
Then to my home above
    I travel calmly on,
And sing, in life or death,
    My Lord, thy will be done!
                                SCHMOLK.

218.   *Trust.*   6s. D.

THY way, not mine, O Lord,
    However dark it be!
Lead me by thine own hand;
    Choose out the path for me.
I dare not choose my lot:
    I would not, if I might;
Choose thou for me, my God,
    So shall I walk aright.

2 Choose thou for me my friends,
    My sickness or my health;

Choose thou my cares for me,
  My poverty or wealth.
Not mine, not mine the choice,
  In things or great or small;
Be thou my Guide, my Strength,
  My Wisdom, and my All. BONAR.

219. *Faith.* L. M.

'TIS by the faith of joys to come
  We walk thro' deserts dark as night;
Till we arrive at heaven, our home,
  Faith is our guide, and faith our light.

2 The want of sight she well supplies;
  She makes the pearly gates appear·
Far into distant worlds she pries,
  And brings eternal glories near.

3 Cheerful we tread the desert through,
  While faith inspires a heavenly ray;
Though lions roar, and tempests blow,
  And rocks and dangers fill the way.
                                WATTS.

220. *God's Peace.*—Phil. iv. 7. C. M.

WE bless thee for thy peace, O God!
  Deep as the boundless sea,
Which falls like sunshine on the road
  Of those who trust in thee.

2 We ask not, Father, for repose
  Which comes from outward rest,
If we may have through all life's woes
  Thy peace within our breast:—

3 That peace which flows serene and deep—
  A river in the soul,

Whose banks a living verdure keep:
God's sunshine o'er the whole!

4 Such, Father, give our hearts such peace,
Whate'er the outward be,
Till all life's discipline shall cease,
And we go home to thee.

SPECIAL OCCASIONS.

221. *Goodness of God in the Seasons.* S. M.

GREAT God, at thy command
Seasons in order rise:
Thy power and love in concert reign
Through earth, and seas, and skies.

2 How balmy is the air!
How warm the sun's bright beams!
While, to refresh the ground, the rains
Descend in gentle streams.

3 With grateful praise we own
Thy kind providing hand,
While grass, and herbs, and waving corn,
Adorn and bless the land.   GIBBONS.

222. *Goodness of Providence.* C. M.

GOD of our lives! thy various praise
Our voices shall resound:
Thy hand revolves our fleeting days
And brings the seasons round.

2 To thee shall daily incense rise,
Our Father and our Friend;

While daily mercies from the skies
  In genial streams descend.

3 In every scene of life, thy care,
  In every age, we see:
And, constant as thy favors are,
  So let our praises be.

4 Still may thy love, in every scene,
  In every age, appear;
And let the same compassion deign
  To bless the opening year.
                            HEGINBOTHAM.

223.   *New Year.*   7s. D.

WHILE, with ceaseless course, the sun
    Hasted through the former year,
Many souls their race have run,
  Nevermore to meet us here:
Fixed in an eternal state,
  They have done with all below;
We a little longer wait;
  But how little none can know.

2 As the winged arrow flies
    Speedily the mark to find;
As the lightning from the skies
  Darts, and leaves no trace behind—
Swiftly thus our fleeting days
  Bear us down life's rapid stream;
Upward, Lord, our spirits raise,
  All below is but a dream.   NEWTON.

224.   *New Year.*   7s

FOR thy mercy and thy grace,
    Constant through another year,
Hear our song of thankfulness:
  Jesus, our Redeemer! hear.

2 In our weakness and distress,
  Rock of Strength! be thou our stay;
In the pathless wilderness,
  Be our true and living way.

3 Who of us death's awful road
  In the coming year shall tread—
With thy rod and staff, O Lord!
  Comfort thou his dying-bed.

4 Make us faithful, make us pure;
  Keep us evermore thine own;
Help thy servants to endure;
  Fit us for the promised crown.

225. *New Year.* L. M.

GREAT God! we sing that mighty hand,
By which supported still we stand:
The opening year thy mercy shows;
That mercy crowns it till it close.

2 By day, by night, at home, abroad,
Still we are guarded by our God;
By his incessant bounty fed,
By his unerring counsel led.

3 With grateful hearts the past we own:
The future, all to us unknown,
We to thy guardian care commit,
And peaceful leave before thy feet.

4 In scenes exalted or depressed,
Be thou our joy, and thou our rest;
Thy goodness all our hopes shall raise,
Adored through all our changing days.

                              DODDRIDGE.

226. *New Year.* C. M.

OUR Father! through the coming year
   We know not what shall be;
But we would leave without a fear
   Its ordering all to thee.

2 It may be we shall toil in vain
   For what the world holds fair;
And all the good we thought to gain,
   Deceive and prove but care.

3 But calmly, Lord, on thee we rest;
   No fears our trust shall move;
Thou knowest what for each is best,
   And thou art Perfect Love.

227. *God's Kindness to our Forefathers.* C. M.

TO Him from whom our blessings flow,
   Who all our wants supplies,
This day the choral song and vow
   From grateful hearts shall rise.

2 'Twas he who led the pilgrim band
   Across the stormy sea;
'Twas he who stayed the tyrant's hand
   And set our country free.

3 When shivering on a strand unknown,
   In sickness and distress,
Our fathers looked to God alone
   To save, protect, and bless.

4 Be thou our nation's strength and shield
   In manhood as in youth;
Thine arm for our protection wield,
   And guide us by thy truth.

I

228. *National.* L. M.

O GOD, beneath thy guiding hand
    Our exiled fathers crossed the sea;
And when they trod the wintry strand,
    With prayer and psalm they worshiped thee.

2 Laws, freedom, truth, and faith in God
    Came with those exiles o'er the waves;
And where their pilgrim feet have trod,
    The God they trusted guards their graves.

3 And here thy name, O God of love,
    Their children's children shall adore,
Till these eternal hills remove,
    And spring adorns the earth no more.
                                    L. BACON.

229. *Our Country.* 6s. & 4s.

GOD bless our native land!
    Firm may she ever stand,
        Through storm and night;
When the wild tempests rave,
Ruler of winds and wave,
Do thou our country save
        By thy great might.

2 For her our prayer shall rise
To God above the skies,
    On him we wait;
Thou who art ever nigh,
Guarding with watchful eye,
To thee aloud we cry,
    God save the State!
                                    J. S. DWIGHT.

230. *Patriotic.* 6s. & 4s.

MY country, 'tis of thee,
    Sweet land of liberty,

Of thee I sing:
Land where my fathers died,
Land of the pilgrim's pride,
From every mountain-side
 Let freedom ring!

2 My native country, thee—
Land of the noble free—
 Thy name I love:
I love thy rocks and rills,
Thy woods and templed hills;
My heart with rapture thrills
 Like that above.

3 Let music swell the breeze,
And ring from all the trees
 Sweet freedom's song!
Let mortal tongues awake;
Let all that breathe partake;
Let rocks their silence break—
 The sound prolong!

4 Our fathers' God! to thee,
Author of liberty,
 To thee we sing:
Long may our land be bright
With freedom's holy light;
Protect us by thy might,
 Great God, our King!

S. F. SMITH.

231.   *The Union.*   L. M. 6l.

WITH grateful hearts, with joyful tongues,
 To God we raise united songs;
His power and mercy we proclaim.
 Our Union bless, and make us own
 Jehovah here has fixed his throne,
And triumph in his mighty name.

2 Long as the moon her course shall run,
Or men behold the circling sun,
Within our borders hold thy reign;
 Crown our just counsels with success,
 With truth and peace our nation bless,
And all our sacred rights maintain.

MORTALITY AND IMMORTALITY.

232. *Brevity of Life.* 7s. & 6s.

TIME is winging us away
 To our eternal home;
Life is but a winter's day—
 A journey to the tomb;
Youth and vigor soon will flee,
 Blooming beauty lose its charms,
All that's mortal soon shall be
 Enclosed in death's cold arms.

2 Time is winging us away
 To our eternal home;
Life is but a winter's day—
 A journey to the tomb;
But the Christian shall enjoy
 Health and beauty soon above,
Far beyond the world's alloy,
 Secure in Jesus' love.   BURTON.

233. *The Pilgrim's Song.* S. M. D.

A FEW more years shall roll,
 A few more seasons come;
And we shall be with those that rest,
 Asleep within the tomb:

Then, O my Lord, prepare
  My soul for that great day;
Oh, wash me in thy precious blood,
  And take my sins away!

2 A few more storms shall beat
  On this wild, rocky shore;
And we shall be where tempests cease,
  And surges swell no more:
Then, O my Lord, prepare
  My soul for that calm day;
Oh, wash me in thy precious blood,
  And take my sins away!

3 A few more struggles here,
  A few more partings o'er,
A few more toils, a few more tears,
  And we shall weep no more:
Then, O my Lord, prepare
  My soul for that blest day;
Oh, wash me in thy precious blood,
  And take my sins away! BONAR.

234. Psalm ciii. 15. L. M.

HOW vain is all beneath the skies!
  How transient every earthly bliss!
How slender all the fondest ties,
  That bind us to a world like this!

2 The evening cloud, the morning dew,
  The withering grass, the fading flower,
Of earthly hopes are emblems true—
  The glory of a passing hour!

3 But though earth's fairest blossoms die,
  And all beneath the skies is vain,
There is a land whose confines lie
  Beyond the reach of care and pain.

4 Then let the hope of joys to come
    Dispel our cares and chase our fears:
If God be ours, we're trav'ling home,
    Though passing through a vale of tears.

235.   *Life Eternal.*   8s. & 7s.

EVERY thing we love and cherish
    Hastens onward to the grave;
Earthly joys and pleasures perish,
    And whate'er the world e'er gave.

2 All is fading, all is fleeing;
    Earthly flames must cease to glow,
Earthly beings cease from being,
    Earthly blossoms cease to blow.

3 Yet unchanged, while all decayeth,
    Jesus stands upon the dust;
"Lean on me alone," he sayeth,
    "Hope and love and firmly trust."

4 Oh, abide, abide with Jesus,
    Who himself forever lives,
Who from death eternal frees us,
    Yea, who life eternal gives.

236.   1 Cor. xv. 19.   S. H. M.

FRIEND after friend departs;
    Who has not lost a friend?
There is no union here of hearts
    That finds not here an end:
Were this frail world our only rest,
Living or dying none were blest.

2 Beyond the flight of time,
    Beyond this vale of death,
There surely is some blessed clime

Where life is not a breath,
Nor life's affections transient fire,
Whose sparks fly upward and expire.

3 There is a world above
　Where parting is unknown;
A whole eternity of love
　Formed for the good alone;
And faith beholds the dying here
Translated to that happier sphere.

4 Thus star by star declines
　Till all are passed away,
As morning high and higher shines
　To pure and perfect day:
Nor sink those stars in empty night;
　They hide themselves in heaven's own
　　light.　　　　MONTGOMERY.

237.　　1 Thess. iv. 14.　　L. M.

ASLEEP in Jesus! blessed sleep!
　From which none ever wake to weep;
A calm and undisturbed repose,
Unbroken by the last of foes.

2 Asleep in Jesus! oh, how sweet
To be for such a slumber meet!
With holy confidence to sing
That death hath lost its venomed sting.

3 Asleep in Jesus! peaceful rest!
Whose waking is supremely blest;
No fear, no woe, shall dim that hour
Which manifests the Saviour's power.

4 Asleep in Jesus! oh, for me
May such a blissful refuge be!

Securely shall my ashes lie,
And wait the summons from on high.
MRS. MACKAY.

238. *Dust to Dust.* C. M.

CALM on the bosom of thy God,
  Young spirit, rest thee now!
Ev'n while with us thy footsteps trod,
  His seal was on thy brow.

2 Dust, to its narrow house beneath!
  Soul, to its place on high!
They that have seen thy look in death
  No more may fear to die.

3 Lone are the paths, and sad the bowers,
  Whence thy meek smile is gone;
But, oh! a brighter home than ours,
  In heaven, is now thine own.
HEMANS.

239. *Home in Heaven.* 6s. & 4s.

I'M but a stranger here,
  Heaven is my home;
Earth is a desert drear,
  Heaven is my home:
Danger and sorrow stand
Round me on every hand,
Heaven is my fatherland—
  Heaven is my home.

2 What though the tempests rage,
  Heaven is my home;
Short is my pilgrimage,
  Heaven is my home:
Time's cold and wintry blast
Soon will be overpast;

I shall reach home at last—
  Heaven is my home.   TAYLOR.

240.   *The Life Above.*   S. M.

OH, where shall rest be found—
  Rest for the weary soul?
'Twere vain the ocean depths to sound,
  Or pierce to either pole.

2 The world can never give
  The bliss for which we sigh:
'Tis not the whole of life to live,
  Nor all of death to die.

3 Beyond this vale of tears
  There is a life above,
Unmeasured by the flight of years;
  And all that life is love.
                MONTGOMERY.

241.   *Aspirations.*   7s. & 6s.

RISE, my soul! and stretch thy wings,
  Thy better portion trace;
Rise from transitory things
  Toward heaven, thy native place:
Sun, and moon, and stars decay,
  Time shall soon this earth remove;
Rise, my soul, and haste away
  To seats prepared above!

2 Rivers to the ocean run,
  Nor stay in all their course;
Fire, ascending, seeks the sun—
  Both speed them to their source:
So a soul that's born of God,
  Pants to view his glorious face,
Upward tends to his abode,
  To rest in his embrace.

3 Cease, ye pilgrims! cease to mourn—
   Press onward to the prize;
Soon your Saviour will return
   Triumphant in the skies:
Yet a season, and you know
   Happy entrance will be given,
All your sorrows left below,
   And earth exchanged for heaven.
CENNICK.

242.   *Light from Afar.*   6s. & 4s.

WHILE on life's stormy sea
   My bark is driven,
From a far coast, to me
   Sweet light is given;
Gleaming around my way,
Changing night into day,
Blending its golden ray
   With hues of heaven.

2 That beacon light I have,
   And lose all fear;
The Saviour walks the wave,
   His voice I hear:
My perfect, precious Guide,
Bidding the storm subside,
Showing beyond the tide
   Skies heavenly clear.

3 I feel thy magnet powers,
   Bright world to come!
Faith sees thy glorious bowers
   Where angels roam:
Where loved ones, gone before,
Now beckon from the shore,
And make me long the more
   For them and home.

HEAVEN.

243. *Going Home.* S. M.

THOUGH in a foreign land,
  We are not far from home;
And nearer to our house above
  We every moment come.

2 His grace will to the end
  Stronger and brighter shine;
Nor present things, nor things to come,
  Shall quench the spark divine.

3 When we in darkness walk,
  Nor feel the heavenly flame,
Then is the time to trust our God,
  And rest upon his name.

4 Soon shall our doubts and fears
  Subside at his control;
His loving-kindness shall break through
  The midnight of the soul.
TOPLADY.

244. John xvii. 24. L. M.

LET me be with thee where thou art,
  My Saviour, my eternal Rest;
Then only will this longing heart
  Be fully and forever blest.

2 Let me be with thee where thou art,
  Thine unveiled glory to behold;
Then only will this wandering heart
  Cease to be false to thee and cold.

3 Let me be with thee where thou art,
  Where spotless saints thy name adore;
Then only will this sinful heart
  Be evil and defiled no more.

4 Let me be with thee where thou art,
  Where none can die, where none remove;
There neither death nor life will part
  Me from thy presence and thy love.

245. *Pilgrim's Song.* 7s. & 6s.

FROM every earthly pleasure,
  From every transient joy,
From every mortal treasure
  That soon will fade and die;
No longer these desiring,
  Upward our wishes tend,
To nobler bliss aspiring,
  And joys that never end.

2 What though we are but strangers
  And sojourners below,
And countless snares and dangers
  Surround the path we go?
Though painful and distressing,
  Yet there's a rest above;
And onward still we're pressing,
  To reach that land of love. DAVIS.

246. *Nearer Home.* S. M.

ONE sweetly solemn thought
  Comes to me o'er and o'er—
Nearer my parting hour am I
  Than e'er I was before.

2 Nearer my Father's house,
  Where many mansions be;
Nearer the throne where Jesus reigns,
  Nearer the crystal sea;

3 Nearer my going home,
  Laying my burden down,

Leaving my cross of heavy grief,
  Wearing my starry crown.

4 Jesus! to thee I cling:
  Strengthen my arm of faith;
Stay near me while my way-worn feet
  Press through the stream of death.
CAREY.

247.   Heb. xi. 16.   C. M.

MY feet are weary with the march
  Over the steep hill-side;
City of God! I fain would see
  Thy peaceful waters glide!

2 My hands are weary, toiling on
  For perishable meat;
City of God! I fain would reach
  Thy glorious mercy-seat!

3 Patience, poor heart! His feet were worn,
  His hands were weary too;
His garments stained, and travel-torn,
  His head wet with the dew.

4 Love thou the path thy Saviour trod,
  And patient wait thy rest;
His holy city thou shalt see,
  Home of the loved and blest!

248.   *Pilgrimage of Life.*   L. M.

WE have no home on earth below,
  And time is short, and heaven is near;
Oh, that our hearts were chastened so,
  That we could live as strangers here:

2 Like pilgrims that have paused an hour
  To rest upon a foreign strand;

       Like banished men, who love to pour
         The praises of their fatherland.

    3 Bright are the flowers that God hath lent
        To bloom beneath the traveller's tread,
      And beautiful the starry host
        He spreadeth o'er the pilgrim's head.

    4 But in the land that's far away,
        There needs no light of sun or moon;
      And flowers that never know decay,
        Along its starless shores are strewn.

249. *Onward and Upward.* L. M.

WE go with the redeemed to taste
    Of joy supreme, that never dies:
  Our feet still press the weary waste,
    Our hearts, our home, are in the skies.

 2 And, oh! while on to Zion's hill
      The toilsome path of life we tread,
    Around us, loving Father, still
      Thy circling wings of mercy spread.

 3 From day to day, from hour to hour,
      Oh, let our rising spirits prove
    The strength of thine almighty power,
      The sweetness of thy saving love!

250. Rev. iii. 11. C. M.

THE roseate hues of early dawn,
    The brightness of the day,
  The crimson of the sunset sky,
    How fast they fade away!

 2 Oh, for the pearly gates of heaven!
      Oh, for the golden floor!

Oh, for the Sun of Righteousness,
  That setteth nevermore!

3 The highest hopes we cherish here,
  How soon they tire and faint!
How many a spot defiles the robe
  That wraps an earthly saint!

4 Oh, for a heart that never sins!
  Oh, for a soul washed white!
Oh, for a voice to praise our King,
  Nor weary day nor night!

251. *God our Guide.* C. M.

OH, what a lonely path were ours,
  Could we, O Father, see
No home of rest beyond it all,
  No guide, no help in thee.

2 But thou art near, and with us still,
  To guide us in the way
That leads along this vale of tears
  To the bright realms of day.

3 There shall thy glory, O our God,
  Break fully on our view;
And we, thy saints, rejoice to find
  That all thy word was true.

252. *The Heavenly Courts.* C. M.

YE golden lamps of heaven! farewell,
  With all your feeble light;
Farewell, thou ever-changing moon,
  Pale empress of the night!

2 And thou refulgent orb of day,
  In brighter flames arrayed,

My soul, that springs beyond thy sphere,
  No more demands thine aid.

3 Ye stars are but the shining dust
  Of my divine abode;
The pavement of those heavenly courts
  Where I shall reign with God.

4 The Father of eternal light
  Shall there his beams display;
Nor shall one moment's darkness mix
  With that unvaried day. DODDRIDGE.

253.   1 Thess. iv. 17.   S. M.

"FOREVER with the Lord!"
  Amen! so let it be:
Life from the dead is in that word;
  'Tis immortality!

2 My Father's house on high,
  Home of my soul! how near,
At times, to faith's aspiring eye,
  Thy golden gates appear!

3 "Forever with the Lord!"
  Father, if 'tis thy will,
The promise of thy gracious word
  Ev'n here to me fulfill.

4 So, when my latest breath
  Shall rend the veil in twain,
By death I shall escape from death,
  And life eternal gain.

5 Knowing "as I am known,"
  How shall I love that word,
And oft repeat before the throne,
  "Forever with the Lord!"
                     MONTGOMERY.

254.   *Joys of Heaven.*   S. M.

OUR toils and conflicts cease
  On Canaan's happy shore!
We there shall dwell in endless peace,
  And never hunger more.

2 There, in celestial strains,
  Enraptured myriads sing;
There love in every bosom reigns,
  For God himself is King.

3 We soon shall join the throng,
  Their pleasure we shall share,
And sing the everlasting song
  With all the ransomed there.
                        KELLY.

255.   *Rest Yonder.*   8s. & 7s.

THIS is not my place of resting—
  Mine's a city yet to come;
Onward to it I am hasting—
  On to my eternal home.

2 In it all is light and glory;
  O'er it shines a nightless day:
Every trace of sin's sad story,
  All the curse hath passed away.

3 There the Lamb, our Shepherd, leads us
  By the streams of life along—
On the freshest pastures feeds us,
  Turns our sighing into song.

4 Soon we pass this desert dreary,
  Soon we bid farewell to pain;
Nevermore are sad or weary,
  Never, never sin again!   BONAR.

256. *Home for the Weary.* C. M.

THERE is an hour of peaceful rest,
  To mourning wanderers given;
There is a tear for souls distressed,
A balm for every wounded breast:
  'Tis found above—in heaven.

2 There is a home for weary souls,
  By sin and sorrow driven—
When tossed on life's tempestuous shoals,
Where storms arise, and ocean rolls,
  And all is drear—but heaven.

3 There faith lifts up her cheerful eye,
  To brighter prospects given;
And views the tempest passing by,
The evening shadows quickly fly,
  And all serene—in heaven.

4 There fragrant flowers immortal bloom,
  And joys supreme are given;
There rays divine disperse the gloom;
Beyond the confines of the tomb
  Appears the dawn of heaven!

TAPPAN.

257. *Heaven.* L. M.

THERE is a land mine eye hath seen
  In visions of enraptured thought,
So bright, that all which spreads between
  Is with its radiant glories fraught;

2 A land, upon whose blissful shore,
  There rests no shadow, falls no stain:
There those who meet shall part no more,
  And those long parted meet again.

3 Its skies are not like earthly skies,
  With varying hues of shade and light;
It hath no need of suns to rise
  To dissipate the gloom of night.

4 There sweeps no desolating wind
  Across that calm, serene abode;
The wanderer there a home may find
  Within the paradise of God.

258.   *No Sin in Heaven.*   C. M.

FAR from these narrow scenes of night
  Unbounded glories rise,
And realms of infinite delight,
  Unknown to mortal eyes.

2 Fair, distant land! could mortal eyes
  But half its charms explore,
How would our spirits long to rise,
  And dwell on earth no more!

3 No clouds those blissful regions know—
  Realms ever bright and fair!
For sin, the source of mortal woe,
  Can never enter there.

4 Oh, may the heavenly prospect fire
  Our hearts with ardent love!
Till wings of faith, and strong desire,
  Bear every thought above.
                              Mrs. Steele.

259.   *The Safe Fold.*   C. M.

THERE is a fold whence none can stray,
  And pastures ever green,
Where sultry sun, or stormy day,
  Or night is never seen.

2 Far up the everlasting hills,
   In God's own light it lies;
His smile its vast dimension fills
   With joy that never dies.

3 One narrow vale, one darksome wave,
   Divides that land from this;
I have a Shepherd, pledged to save
   And bear me home to bliss.

4 Soon at his feet my soul will lie,
   In life's last struggling breath;
But I shall only seem to die,
   I shall not taste of death.

5 Far from this guilty world,
   Exempt from toil and strife;
To spend eternity with thee,
   My Saviour, this is life!

260. Rev. xxi., xxii. S. M. D.

THERE is no night in heaven;
   In that blest world above
Work never can bring weariness,
   For work itself is love.
There is no grief in heaven;
   For life is one glad day,
And tears are of those former things
   Which all have passed away.

2 There is no sin in heaven;
   Behold that blessed throng!
All holy is their spotless robe,
   All holy is their song.
There is no death in heaven;
   For they who gain that shore
Have won their immortality,
   And they can die no more.

261. *Home Above.* S. M.

I HAVE a home above,
  From sin and sorrow free;
A mansion which eternal love
  Designed and formed for me.

2 My Father's gracious hand
  Has built this sweet abode;
From everlasting it was planned—
  My dwelling-place with God.

3 Loved ones are gone before,
  Whose pilgrim days are done:
I soon shall greet them on that shore
  Where parting is unknown.

262. John xvii. 24. 7s. & 6s.

NO seas again shall sever,
  No desert intervene,
No deep, sad-flowing river
  Shall roll its tide between:
Love and unsevered union
  Of soul with those we love,
Nearness and glad communion,
  Shall be our joy above.

2 No dread of wasting sickness,
  No thought of ache or pain,
No fretting hours of weakness,
  Shall mar our peace again:
No death, our homes o'ershading,
  Shall e'er our harps unstring;
For all is life unfading
  In presence of our King! BONAR.

263.   *The New Jerusalem.*   C. M.

JERUSALEM, Jerusalem!
  Name ever dear to me!
Oh, may at last my home be found,
  City of God, in thee.

2 Oh, may these eyes thy crystal walls
  And gates of pearl behold,
Thy jasper and thy sapphire stones,
  Thy streets of purest gold.

3 The alleluia of thy hymns,
  Before the great I Am!
The harpers harping with their harps,
  The new song of the Lamb!

4 The white robes of thy ransomed hosts,
  The victor palms they bear;
Prophets, apostles, martyrs, saints,
  Dear friends and kindred there!

5 Jerusalem, Jerusalem!
  Name ever dear to me!
Oh, may at last my home be found,
  City of God, in thee!

264.   *Life Eternal.*   7s. & 6s.

BRIEF life is here our portion,
  Brief sorrow, short-lived care;
The life that knows no ending,
  The tearless life is there.
O happy retribution!
  Short toil, eternal rest;
For mortals and for sinners,
  A mansion with the blest.

2 And they who, with their Leader,
   Have conquered in the fight,
Forever and forever
   Are clad in robes of white.
O land that seest no sorrow!
   O state that fear'st no strife!
O royal land of flowers!
   O realm and home of life!
        BERNARD, by DR. NEALE.

265.   *The New Jerusalem.*   7s. & 6s.

JERUSALEM, the golden!
   With milk and honey blest;
Beneath thy contemplation
   Sink heart and voice oppressed.
I know not, oh! I know not
   What joys await me there;
What radiancy of glory,
   What bliss beyond compare.

2 O one, O only mansion!
   O Paradise of joy!
Where tears are ever banished,
   And smiles have no alloy;
Thou hast no shores, fair ocean!
   Thou hast no time, bright day!
Dear fountain of refreshment
   To pilgrims far away.
        BERNARD, by DR. NEALE.

266.   *My Father's House.*   C. M.

THERE is a place of waveless rest,
   Far, far beyond the skies,
Where beauty smiles eternally,
   And pleasure never dies.

2 My Father's house, my heavenly home!
   Where "many mansions" stand,
Prepared by hands divine for all
   Who seek the "better land."

3 When tossed upon the waves of life,
   With fear on every side,
When fiercely howls the gathering storm,
   And foams the angry tide—

4 Beyond the storm, beyond the gloom,
   Breaks forth the light of morn,
Bright beaming from my Father's house,
   To cheer the soul forlorn.

CHANTS.

1.   *The Lord's Prayer.*

OUR FATHER which art in heaven,
  Hallowed be thy name;
Thy kingdom come,
  Thy will be done in earth, as it is in heaven.
Give us this day our daily bread; and forgive
      us our debts,
  As we forgive our debtors;
And lead us not into temptation,
  But deliver us from evil;
For thine is the kingdom, and the power, and
      the glory,
  Forever. Amen.

2.   Psalm xxiii.

THE Lord is my shepherd; I shall not
   want.

2 He maketh me to lie down in green pastures:
  He leadeth me beside the still waters.

3 He restoreth my soul:
  He leadeth me in the paths of righteousness for his name's sake.

4 Yea, though I walk through the valley of the shadow of death, I will fear no evil;
  For thou art with me: thy rod and thy staff they comfort me.

5 Thou preparest a table before me in the presence of mine enemies:

Thou anointest my head with oil; my cup runneth over.

6 Surely goodness and mercy shall follow me all the days of my life:
And I will dwell in the house of the Lord forever.

3. Psalm xcv.

OH, come, let us sing unto the Lord:
Let us heartily rejoice in the strength of our salvation.

2 Let us come before his presence with thanksgiving,
And show ourselves glad in him with psalms.

3 For the Lord is a great God;
And a great King above all gods.

4 In his hand are all the corners of the earth;
And the strength of the hills is his also.

5 The sea is his, and he made it;
And his hands prepared the dry land.

6 Oh, come, let us worship and fall down,
And kneel before the Lord our Maker.

7 For he is the Lord our God;
And we are the people of his pasture, and the sheep of his hand.

8 Oh, worship the Lord in the beauty of holiness;
Let the whole earth stand in awe of him.

9 For he cometh, for he cometh to judge the earth;
And with righteousness to judge the world, and the people with his truth.

4.   Psalm ciii.

PRAISE the Lord, O my soul:
  And all that is within me praise his holy name.
2 Praise the Lord, O my soul;
  And forget not all his benefits.
3 Who forgiveth all thy sin;
  And healeth all thine infirmities.
4 Who saveth thy life from destruction,
  And crowneth thee with mercy and loving-kindness.
5 Oh, praise the Lord, ye angels of his, ye that excel in strength:
  Ye that fulfill his commandment, and hearken unto the voice of his word.
6 Oh, praise the Lord, all ye his hosts;
  Ye servants of his that do his pleasure.
7 Oh, speak good of the Lord, all ye works of his, in all places of his dominion;
  Praise thou the Lord, O my soul.

5.   Psalm ciii.

THE Lord is merciful and gracious,
  Slow to anger, and abundant in mercy.
2 He will not always chide;
  Neither will he keep his anger forever.
3 He hath not dealt with us after our sins,
  Nor rewarded us according to our iniquities.
4 For as the heaven is high above the earth,
  So great is his mercy toward them that fear him.

5 As far as the east is from the west,
   So far hath he removed our transgressions from us.

6 Like as a father pitieth his children,
   So the Lord pitieth them that fear him.

7 For he knoweth our frame;
   He remembereth that we are dust.

6.   Psalm cxxi.

I WILL lift up mine eyes unto the hills,
   From whence cometh my help.

2 My help cometh from the Lord,
   Which made heaven and earth.

3 He will not suffer thy foot to be moved:
   He that keepeth thee will not slumber.

4 Behold, he that keepeth Israel
   Shall not slumber nor sleep.

5 The Lord is thy keeper;
   The Lord is thy shade upon thy right hand.

6 The sun shall not smite thee by day,
   Nor the moon by night.

7 The Lord shall preserve thee from all evil;
   He shall preserve thy soul.

8. The Lord shall preserve thy going out, and thy coming in,
   From this time forth, and even forevermore.

INDEX OF FIRST LINES.

	HYMN
A few more years shall roll	233
A glory gilds the sacred page	103
Abide with me! fast falls the eventide	24
All ye nations, praise the Lord	38
Almighty God, in humble prayer	163
Always with us, always with us	132
Asleep in Jesus! blessed sleep!	237
As with gladness men of old	182
Author of good! to thee we turn	173
Awake, and sing the song	116
Awake, my soul, and with the sun	4
Awake, my soul, to joyful lays	118
Awake, my soul! stretch every nerve	202
Awake, my tongue! thy tribute bring	52
Awake, our souls! away, our fears!	203
Away from earth my spirit turns	130
Begin, my soul, th' exalted lay	41
Behold the throne of grace!	196
Behold, where in a mortal form	112
Blest are the pure in heart	209
Blest be thou, O God of Israel	36
Brief life is here our portion	264
Brightest and best of the sons of the morning	108
Call Jehovah thy salvation	89
Calm on the bosom of thy God	238
Calm on the listening ear of night	109
Christ, whose glory fills the skies	129
Come, gracious Spirit, heavenly dove	195
Come, Jesus, Redeemer, abide thou with me	137
Come, let us lift our joyful eyes	46
Come, let us to the Lord, our God	207
Come, my soul, thy suit prepare	188

Index of First Lines.

	HYMN
Come, O my soul, in sacred lays	53
Come, said Jesus' sacred voice	213
Come, sound his praise abroad	49
Come, thou Almighty King	40
Come unto me, when shadows darkly gather	135
Come, we who love the Lord	212
Come, ye that know and fear the Lord	80
Dear Father, to thy mercy-seat	178
Every human tie may perish	84
Every thing we love and cherish	235
Far from these narrow scenes of night	258
Father, hear the prayer we offer!	162
Father in heaven, to whom our hearts	191
Father of light! conduct my feet	159
Father of love and power	16
Father of mercies, in thy word	105
Father, once more let grateful praise	29
Father, thy paternal care	98
Father, whate'er of earthly bliss	179
For a season called to part	27
For thy mercy and thy grace	224
Forever with the Lord!	253
Forth in thy name, O Lord, we go	9
Friend after friend departs	236
From every earthly pleasure	245
Gently, Lord, oh, gently lead us	161
Give thanks to God most high	47
Give to our God immortal praise	33
Glad hearts to thee we bring	45
Glory to God on high!	120
God bless our native land!	229
God is love! his mercy brightens	79
God is my strong salvation	97
God of almighty power	65
God of mercy! God of love!	165
God of our lives! thy various praise	222
God of the morning, at thy voice	3
God of the morning ray	1

Index of First Lines.

	HYMN
God, that madest earth and heaven	20
Go up, go up, my heart!	215
Gracious God, our heavenly Father!	13
Gracious Spirit, Love divine!	194
Grant us, dear Lord, from evil ways	177
Great God, at thy command	221
Great God, my father and my friend	148
Great God! we sing that mighty hand	225
Great source of unexhausted good!	71
Guide me, O thou great Jehovah	154
Hail, tranquil hour of closing day!	15
Hark! what mean those holy voices	107
Heavenly Father, sovereign Lord	39
"He leadeth me!" Oh, blessed thought	93
Holy and reverend is the name	66
Holy Father, thou hast taught me	151
How firm a foundation, ye saints of the Lord!	138
How gentle God's commands	72
How precious is the book divine	104
How shall the young secure their hearts	102
How sweet the name of Jesus sounds	115
How sweetly flowed the gospel sound	113
How vain is all beneath the skies	234
I bow my forehead to the dust	81
I feel within a want	181
I have a home above	261
I heard the voice of Jesus say	136
I'm but a stranger here	239
I sing the almighty power of God	58
I stand on Zion's mount	96
If through unruffled seas	214
In heavenly love abiding	76
In the morning I will pray	7
In vain I trace creation o'er	172
Jehovah! by thy covenant	157
Jehovah, God! thy gracious power	55
Jerusalem, Jerusalem!	263
Jerusalem, the golden!	265
Jesus, I love thy charming name	122

Index of First Lines.

	HYMN
Jesus, in sickness and in pain	185
Jesus! lover of my soul	189
Jesus, most holy	166
Jesus, our best-beloved Friend	188
Jesus, Shepherd of the sheep	180
Jesus, still lead on	184
Jesus, who knows full well	197
Joyful be the hours to-day	121
Keep us, Lord, oh, keep us ever	156
Know, my soul, thy full salvation	204
Lamp of our feet, whereby we trace	106
Lead us heavenly Father, lead us	192
Let me be with Thee where thou art	244
Lift up to God the voice of praise	30
Lord, as to thy dear Cross we flee	134
Lord, I address thy heavenly throne	146
Lord, in the morning thou shalt hear	6
Lord, in thy great, thy glorious name	152
Lord, it is not life to live	190
Lord of earth! thy forming hand	99
Lord, thou hast searched and seen me through	64
Lord, we have wandered forth	153
Lord, when we bend before thy throne	167
Love divine, all love excelling	149
Majestic sweetness sits enthroned	114
Make us, by thy transforming grace	111
My country! 'tis of thee	230
My dear Redeemer and my Lord	110
My faith looks up to thee	125
My feet are weary with the march	247
My God, accept my heart this day	176
My God, how endless is thy love!	12
My God, my Father, blissful name!	164
My God, my King, thy various praise	43
My God, thy boundless love I praise	78
My Jesus, as thou wilt	217
My Maker and my King	73
My soul, be on thy guard	201

Index of First Lines.

	HYMN
My soul, repeat His praise	67
My spirit on thy care	216
Nearer, my God, to thee	145
New every morning is the love	14
No change of time shall ever shock	92
No seas again shall sever	262
Now that the sun is gleaming bright	11
Now the shades of night are gone	5
O Father, lift our souls above	170
O for a heart to praise my God	169
O for a shout of joy	82
O God, beneath thy guiding hand	228
O God, my strength, my hope	193
O gracious God, in whom I live	158
O Lord, I would delight in thee	85
O my Saviour, guardian true	21
O that the Lord would guide my ways	147
O thou, from whom all goodness flows	175
O thou, who hast at thy command	174
Oh, bless the Lord, my soul!	50
Oh, cease, my wandering soul	95
Oh, could I speak the matchless worth	126
Oh, happy is the man that hears	210
Oh, help us, Lord, each hour of need	150
Oh, what a lonely path were ours	251
Oh, where shall rest be found	240
Oh, worship the King all-glorious above	57
Once more, my soul, the rising day	2
One sweetly solemn thought	246
One there is above all others	119
Oppressed with noonday's scorching heat	133
Our Father, God, who art in heaven	160
Our Father, through the coming year	226
Our toils and conflicts cease	254
Pilgrims in this vale of sorrow	206
Praise and thanks and cheerful love	44
Praise the Lord, when blushing morning	37
Praise the Lord, who reigns above	35
Praise the Lord! ye heavens, adore him	31

L

Index of First Lines.

	HYMN
Praise to God, immortal praise	34
Praise to thee, thou great Creator	32
Rise, my soul, and stretch thy wings	241
Saviour, breathe an evening blessing	22
Saviour, like a shepherd lead us	187
Saviour, source of every blessing	131
Saviour! thy gentle voice	183
Shine on our souls, eternal God	26
Since all the varying scenes of time	75
Softly now the light of day	18
Still with thee, O my God	25
Sun of my soul, thou Saviour dear	23
Suppliant, low thy children bend	10
Sweet hour of prayer	200
Sweet is the work, my God, my King	48
Sweet peace of conscience, heavenly guest	205
Sweeter to Jesus when on earth	124
Take my heart, O Father, take it!	163
The Lord himself, the mighty Lord	144
The Lord is King! lift up thy voice	54
The Lord is my Shepherd, how happy	141
The Lord is my Shepherd, no want	142
The Lord Jehovah reigns	59
The Lord my pasture shall prepare	140
The pity of the Lord	70
The roseate hues of early dawn	250
There is a fold whence none can stray	259
There is an hour of peaceful rest	256
There is a land mine eye hath seen	257
There is a place of waveless rest	266
There is no night in heaven	260
There's not a star whose twinkling light	62
There's nothing bright above, below	61
They who on the Lord rely	94
They who seek the throne of grace	199
Thine forever, God of love!	155
This curious frame, these noble powers	77
This is not my place of resting	255

Index of First Lines.

	HYMN
Thou art, O God, the life and light...............	60
Thou art the Way, to thee alone..................	128
Thou from whom we never part...................	19
Thou hidden love of God.........................	83
Thou, O Lord, wilt never leave me................	91
Thou, who dwell'st enthroned above...............	51
Though faint, yet pursuing.......................	139
Though in a foreign land.........................	243
Through the day thy love has spared us...........	17
Thy goodness, Lord, our souls confess.............	69
Thy home is with the humble, Lord!..............	208
Thy mighty working, mighty God..................	56
Thy presence, everlasting God....................	28
Thy way, not mine, O Lord......................	218
Time is winging us away.........................	232
'Tis by the faith of joys to come..................	219
'Tis by thy strength the mountains stand..........	63
To heaven I lift my waiting eyes..................	87
To him, from whom our blessings flow............	227
To our Redeemer's glorious name.................	117
To thee, O blessed Saviour.......................	127
To thy pastures, fair and large...................	186
Triumphant Lord, thy goodness reigns............	63
Try us, O God, and search the ground............	171
Up to the hills I lift mine eyes...................	86
Upward I lift mine eyes..........................	88
Vainly through night's weary hours...............	101
We bless thee for thy peace, O God!..............	220
We go with the redeemed to taste.................	249
We have no home on earth below.................	248
When all thy mercies, O my God..................	74
Where wilt thou put thy trust....................	97
While my Redeemer's near.......................	143
While on life's stormy sea........................	242
While our days on earth are lengthened...........	8
While thee I seek, protecting Power!..............	211
While with ceaseless course the sun...............	223
Whom have we, Lord, in heaven but thee?.........	100

Index of First Lines.

HYMN
With grateful hearts, with joyful tongues........... 231
With joy we meditate the grace.................... 123

Ye golden lamps of heaven! farewell............... 252
Yes, I will bless thee, O my God....,.............. 43

www.ingramcontent.com/pod-product-compliance
Lightning Source LLC
Chambersburg PA
CBHW030251170426
43202CB00009B/706